GORDON
RAMSAY

TOP CHEFS

TOP CHEFS

GORDON
RAMSAY

ANNETTE GALIOTO

Produced by OTTN Publishing, Stockton, New Jersey

Eldorado Ink
PO Box 100097
Pittsburgh, PA 15233
www.eldoradoink.com

CPSIA compliance information: Batch#TC010112-6. For further
information, contact Eldorado Ink at info@eldoradoink.com.

First printing

1 3 5 7 9 8 6 4 2

Library of Congress Cataloging-in-Publication Data

Galioto, Annette.
 Gordon Ramsay / by Annette Galioto.
     p. cm. — (Top chefs)
 Includes bibliographical references and index.
 ISBN 978-1-61900-022-3 (hc)
 ISBN 978-1-61900-023-0 (pb)
 ISBN 978-1-61900-024-7 (ebook)
 1. Ramsay, Gordon—Juvenile literature. 2. Cooks—Great Britain—
Biography. 3. Celebrity chefs—Great Britain—Biography. I. Title.
 TX649.R26G35 2012
 641.5092—dc23
 [B]
                                          2011044850

For information about custom editions, special sales, or
premiums, please contact our special sales department at
info@eldoradoink.com.

TABLE OF CONTENTS

Celebrity chef Gordon Ramsay makes a dramatic entrance on his hit reality show *Hell's Kitchen*. Gordon has an intimidating reputation as a perfectionist who will not hesitate to criticize any cook whose work does not meet his high standards.

CHAPTER ONE

TRIAL BY FIRE

In early 2008, 15 men and women filed onto a bus taking them from the Los Angeles airport to a television production studio in Culver City, California. They were contestants in the competitive reality TV cooking show *Hell's Kitchen*. The program, broadcast by Fox Television, was filming its fourth season.

During the bus ride, some of the contestants talked about the show's host, celebrity chef Gordon Ramsay. "Chef Ramsay is going to eat you alive," warned one. Others bragged about their cooking skills and how they were going to win the competition.

When the contestants arrived at the studio, they did not see the show's host. Instead, they were greeted by Jean-Philippe Susilovic, the French maître d' of the reality show's restaurant. The new arrivals then received a big surprise. One of the contestants who had been riding with them in the bus began to remove a wig and a mask. Beneath the disguise was Gordon Ramsay. Not only had he heard all the negative things they said about him, but he also knew which ones had boasted of being great chefs. And he was about to prove them wrong.

THE VOLATILE CHEF

As host of *Hell's Kitchen*, Ramsay presents a variety of cooking challenges to contestants. Over the course of the season, he judges their efforts, criticizes their results, and determines who stays and who goes.

At the beginning of each season, the cooks take on their first task. They are each allowed 45 minutes to prepare their tastiest, signature dish and then present it to Ramsay for judgment. Afterward, the participants work as members of one of two teams, and the teams compete against each other in cooking challenges. When Gordon decides there is a winning team, its members receive a reward, such as a helicopter ride over Los Angeles or dinner out on Ramsay's yacht. The losing team is assigned tasks such as kitchen duty, decorating a restaurant, or making and serving a dinner to the winning team.

But pleasing the judge is hard. Gordon has a well-deserved reputation for being demanding and difficult. The temperamental chef, who stands six foot two inches tall, is an imposing figure who typically looms over most of the contestants. If

A signature dish, like someone's signature on a paper, is unique and identifies the personality and style of a chef.

COMPETING ON *HELL'S KITCHEN*

Hundreds of hopeful contestants flock to Hell's Kitchen casting calls, which are typically held in major cities across the country. Aspiring contestants have to fill out an 11-page application, in which they answer questions such as, "How do you react to criticism?" and "Describe your relationship with your parents." Some applicants are subjected to medical, psychological, or background investigations. They must be willing to work long hours in hot and sometimes dangerous conditions.

Once selected to appear on the program, contestants have to give up five to six weeks of their lives. During that time, they share a bedroom with three or four strangers in a dormitory, where the cameras are always filming. Work typically starts at 7 A.M. and ends at 2 A.M.—after dinner service and after the kitchen has been washed and cleaned. In addition to these hardships, they daily face a tyrannical head chef with a reputation for verbally beating contestants into submission.

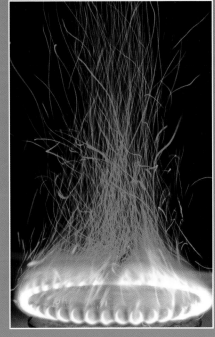

It can be even more stressful because reality television programs keep contestants isolated during filming. Jen Yemola, who was in the 2007 season of *Hell's Kitchen*, told the *New York Times* that before production started, "They locked me in a hotel room for three or four days. They took all my books, my CDs, my phone, any newspapers. I was allowed to leave the room only with an escort. It was like I was in prison."

Gordon berates several members of the red team on an episode of Hell's Kitchen. The popular show has aired on the Fox network since 2005.

Ramsay doesn't like what he sees, his piercing blue eyes squint into narrow slits, his lips curl and snarl, and his face turns red. He lashes out with outbursts and insults couched in choice curse words. With his slashing tongue and diabolic manner, Gordon becomes a fire-breathing chef who intimidates even the bravest of cooks. When Season 4 of *Hell's Kitchen* rolled around, the contestants knew what to expect from its volatile host. And he delivered.

RUBBER CHICKEN

In the first episode, the competing chefs were to prepare an entire meal for hungry diners at the Hell's Kitchen restaurant. Gordon was unhappy that it took a long time for the contestants to serve the appetizers. And when he checked the entree, his seething turned into a full boil. "Who cooked the chicken?" he demanded. "It's rubber!" he screamed as he hurled it ferociously into a wall. The disheartened chefs scurried back to their dorms (during the six weeks of filming, contestants live onsite), and the restaurant patrons were sent home hungry.

The tongue-lashing didn't stop there. The following morning the contestants were booted out of bed at 5:43 A.M., as sous chefs Scott Leibfried and Gloria Felix bellowed through bullhorns for the sleepy contestants to get up, and "Get dressed! Go, go, go!" Ramsay stood before the disoriented men and women as they gathered outside the kitchen, and a

Hell's Kitchen is seen in more than 30 countries around the world.

When Hell's Kitchen *first aired in the United States in 2005, Gordon was often compared to Simon Cowell, another British celebrity. Cowell, who at the time was a judge on the Fox show* American Idol, *became famous in the U.S. thanks largely to his often-harsh comments directed at* Idol *contestants.*

trash truck was called over. He proceeded to reprimand the group for wasting so much food, and he informed them that their next chore was to be very unpleasant. He explained, "Now every rubber chicken breast, every overcooked risotto, every rock hard potato you binned last night, get out and put it back in the cylinder."

The hapless contestants had to dig with their bare hands through smelly, slimy trash bags and pull out all the food that had been thrown out the previous evening. They placed it in clear bins, so the amount of wasted food could be seen. The filled containers provided a stark image of how much money a restaurant can lose when a chef is careless with food.

TESTED AND TRIED

Under Ramsay's critical gaze, both amateurs and highly experienced cooks are sorely tested and tried. It takes a brave soul to jump into the fire of *Hell's Kitchen*. But hundreds answer the casting calls, held in cities across the nation, hoping to earn the program's grand prize. The winner gets the chance to serve as head chef at a prestigious restaurant—and typically earn a salary of around $250,000. Season 4 contestants were competing for the opportunity to run Ramsay's new L.A. restaurant—Gordon Ramsay at the London West Hollywood—scheduled to open that May.

As in most reality show competitions, the contestants vote on who should be eliminated from *Hell's Kitchen*. But Ramsay is the final judge when it comes to booting off contestants and in determining the winner of the show. Most critics attribute the show's success to his passion for perfection as well as his volatile personality.

Ramsay is much more than a TV celebrity. He is also a celebrated chef, having earned 12 Michelin star ratings. (Being awarded a Michelin star is the highest honor for chefs.) He is also a multimillionaire—the owner of a vast restaurant empire, the author of more than 20 cookbooks, and a businessman who has made many lucrative licensing agreements. But most of all, he is a culinary perfectionist who is passionate about food, and whose drive to become the greatest chef in the world led him to success.

CHAPTER TWO

DRIVEN TO SUCCEED

Gordon did not always want to be a chef. His first dream was to be a professional athlete. The Scottish-born boy had an early love for soccer (which in Europe is known as football). Ramsay had dreams of playing for the football club Glasgow Rangers, in Scotland.

A TOUGH CHILDHOOD

Gordon James Ramsay was born on November 8, 1966, in Johnstone, Renfrewshire, just outside the city of Glasgow. His parents, Helen and Gordon Ramsay, named their first son after his father. Young Gordon was the second of four children. He had an older sister, Diane, and would soon be joined by a brother, Ronnie, and another sister, Yvonne.

Although born in Scotland, Gordon Ramsay grew up in England. Gordon's father worked many different jobs, from swimming pool manager, to welder, to band musician. But he was a heavy drinker and had a fiery temper, and he seldom held any job for long. When his debts grew too big, he packed the family in the van and they moved. Gordon has said that his family lived in about 17 different places as he was growing up.

From around the age of five, Gordon lived in the area around Stratford-upon-Avon, a quaint market town in England. However, the Ramsays didn't live in the tourist part of the town. Gordon would grow up in council estates, the British term for low-income housing subsidized by the local government. Because of Gordon senior's unstable ways, his family lived in poverty.

The elder Gordon was also physically abusive to his wife and children. But Helen stayed in the marriage and tried to

The town of Stratford-upon-Avon, where Gordon Ramsay grew up, is famous as the birthplace of the playwright William Shakespeare. More than 3 million tourists visit Stratford each year to see the house where Shakespeare lived, above. Few visitors, however, see the low-income housing projects where the Ramsay family lived in the 1970s.

protect the children from his tirades. Gordon described the domestic violence:

> I watched how he battled alcoholism and how he became terribly violent with my mum, to the point where she feared for her life. Every time he got violent, any present that my brother, sisters, or I had given mum would be smashed, simply because he knew it belonged to her. There were instances when the police were called to take him away; mum was taken to the hospital while we kids were taken to a children's home.

The elder Ramsay was also mentally cruel to his wife and children. He bullied Gordon, making him feel inadequate. It was a difficult childhood. "As a boy, I was often afraid and ashamed, and always poor," Gordon would later say.

Gordon found that attempts to please his father typically brought more harsh criticism. It was clear to the boy and his sisters that the senior Ramsay favored his younger son. "Ronnie was always Dad's blue-eyed boy." Gordon would later say, "He was Number One. Definitely the favourite."

SOCCER PHENOM

In a failed effort to jumpstart a music career, the senior Gordon spent most of the family's money on band instruments. When he got music gigs, he often pressured his children to perform alongside him.

Young Gordon wasn't musically inclined, but he had talents as an athlete. At eight years old he could not only kick a ball with tremendous accuracy and force but also easily maneuver it wherever he wanted it to go. He realized that one way to gain his father's approval was by becoming good enough to play for the Glasgow Rangers, his father's favorite team. Over the years, the boy worked hard to improve his talents on the soccer field.

At the age of 15 Gordon left school and signed up for several semi-professional soccer teams. He was playing for Oxford United in 1981, when he was spotted by a scout for the Glasgow Rangers. The scout invited Gordon to take a trip back to Glasgow to try out for the team.

After competing in the trials, Gordon returned home, where he waited anxiously for news. Four weeks later he got a letter asking if he would like to train as an apprentice. The offer included the possibility that after a year he could become a reserve-team player on the youth squad.

RANGERS FOOTBALL CLUB

To support his son's soccer career with the Rangers, Gordon Ramsay senior moved the family back to Glasgow. Gordon would later say that he felt strong pressure to succeed, as if the responsibility for his family's future happiness rested on his shoulders. The situation at home was tense, as the relationship between his parents was deteriorating. Through it all, Gordon worked to concentrate on his training, which went well.

Then, in 1984, Gordon's knee was injured during a training session. He continued to play through the pain for the

The most famous Scottish football club (FC) is the Rangers FC. Founded in 1872, the team plays at Ibrox Stadium in Glasgow.

Gordon's dreams of playing soccer for the Glasgow Rangers were ended by injuries to his knee.

rest of the day. But when he finally went to the hospital, he was told he had damaged the cartilage in his knee and would have to stop playing so the injury could heal. It took 11 weeks to recover.

Soon after his knee was declared mended, Gordon began training hard in an effort to get back in shape as quickly as possible. But a few weeks later, while playing a game of squash, he tore a cruciate ligament (connective tissue that crosses the knee joint and connects the femur, or thigh bone, to the tibia, or lower leg bone).

This was a much more serious injury that required him to wear a cast on his leg for the next four months. When the cast came off, Gordon again focused on his training. But the knee injuries had taken a toll, and he was not playing as well as he had before. In 1985, at the start of the next playing season, the club manager and assistant called Gordon into their office. They told Gordon that he was being cut from the team. They suggested that he get physical therapy with the goal of signing with a lower league team, and eventually trying to work his way back up to the Rangers.

Gordon's reply was immediate, "I said no, straight away. I'm an all-or-nothing guy and I knew that, if I couldn't play for Rangers, then forget it." He would later write how the news affected him:

> I went home, sat down and finally started to cry . . . I was too upset to talk to anyone and bawled my eyes out in private for the whole weekend. I thought, Christ, that's it. All my mates know. What do I do now? The sense of rejection was humiliating, awful, and I took the failure very, very badly, like any 18-year-old would. I couldn't move on and I wanted to forget about it.

A New Direction

Ramsay left soccer behind and looked for a new way to earn a living. His options were limited. Because he had put all his energy into becoming a professional soccer player, he had no education. He applied for work with the police and with the Royal Navy. But he was not accepted.

In need of money, Gordon finally landed a job with the help of his sister Diane, who was waitressing in a hotel in Stratford-Upon-Avon. The position was as an apprentice cook in the hotel's restaurant. "I loved it instantly, big time," he would later admit. "The boisterousness, the hassle, the shouting, the screaming, the activity. I found a sense of freedom there."

Unfortunately, the senior Gordon Ramsay was not at all supportive of his son's new career. He wanted Gordon to keep playing soccer. Realizing that his father had no respect for the profession he had chosen, Gordon moved out of the family home and took an apartment with his sister Diane in Banbury, a town about 20 miles away from Stratford-upon-Avon.

A few years later Gordon would receive a phone call from Ronnie telling him that their father had beaten up their mother so badly that she had been hospitalized. At the hospital, she was referred to Women's Aid, a charity organization that helps battered women. Rather than return to her husband, she went to live in a Women's Aid shelter for a time before beginning divorce proceedings and finding a new place to live.

After his mother's brutal beating Gordon would let his father know that he no longer wanted anything to do with him. The senior Gordon Ramsay would disappear from the lives of his wife and children. Still, Helen had stayed with her abusive husband for 22 years before she finally grew strong enough to leave him.

In 2007 Gordon Ramsay became an ambassador for Women's Aid, a national charity in England that works to end domestic violence against women and children. He helps raise awareness and funds for the U.K. charity, which helps more than 320,000 women and children each year.

BECOMING A CHEF

While Gordon lived in Banbury, he worked hard at his training as a chef. Some of the hotel staff he worked with saw his enthusiasm and encouraged him to attend classes at a catering school. He enrolled in a hotel-management program at North Oxon Technical College in Banbury, and found fulfillment during an internship in a restaurant kitchen. "There was nothing like it," he later said. "I loved the atmosphere, the boisterousness. I said to my tutor, 'I want to be a chef.'"

In 1987 Ramsay received his higher national diploma (HND) in hotel management. Eager to increase his cooking skills, he worked at several different restaurants to gain experience. He would later say that failing to make the Glasgow Rangers team motivated him to do well as a chef. "I was obsessed with never again being told that I'm not good enough," he wrote. "I had failed once in life. I swore I would never fail at anything ever again."

After a time, Gordon decided he wanted to move up from hotel dining to fine dining. This meant learning haute cuisine—the skillful preparation and cooking of high quality food, typically in the style of traditional and elaborate French cuisine. (*Haute cuisine* is French for "high cooking.")

The best haute cuisine chefs, or master chefs, typically worked in major cities, such as New York, London, and Paris. The best of them held Michelin star ratings for their restaurants, which indicates their work is of outstanding quality. Gordon realized that to train with a master chef, he would need to move to London.

CHAPTER THREE

LEARNING FROM THE BEST

Ramsay arrived in London in 1985 with no contacts but with a strong desire to find a job. After landing a position at the Intercontinental Hotel in Mayfair, he saw one of Britain's most prestigious chefs—Marco Pierre White. His first thought, he would later say, was, "I want to go and work for that guy." The following year, he managed to do just that. He convinced White to hire him to work in the restaurant kitchen of Harvey's.

HARVEY'S

In 1986 White was just 26 years old, but he was already hailed as a culinary genius. He had won numerous awards at his London restaurant, which offered dishes based on French cooking.

Gordon started out at Harvey's as a commis chef, tasked with chopping vegetables. Under White's tutelage, he was soon introduced to hundreds of different kinds of gourmet foods. These included truffles and morels—specialty funguses unique to gourmet cooking—as well as caviar and foie gras. White taught Ramsay the secret to reduced sauces and how to perfectly cook various foods. "In the beginning, I admired Marco more than I can say." Gordon has said. "[H]is cooking left me speechless: the lightness, the control, the fact that everything was made to order. In the kitchen there'd be six portions of beef, or sea bass, or tagliatelle, not fifty. Everything was so fresh, everything was made to order."

Like Ramsay, White had not had experience with gourmet foods while growing up. He too had known poverty and lived in a council estate, although in the city of Leeds. But that shared background did not mean White gave Ramsay any special treatment. The executive chef had a reputation for being harsh to his workers. Gordon worked 17 hours or more each day, with no breaks, and with very little pay. But he

Celebrity chef Marco Pierre White (right) prepares a pasta dish with assistant chef Gordon Ramsay at Harvey's restaurant in London, late 1980s. At the time White was considered London's top young chef, although Gordon would eventually become an even bigger celebrity then his mentor.

thrived under the pressure as his skills were slowly honed and perfected.

Ramsay has often said that a chef has to learn how to take insults and abuse. "The trick is to remember that none of the insults is meant to be personal," he advises. Abusive treatment is common in high-pressure kitchens. "I've been

KITCHEN PECKING ORDER

An aspiring chef must move up the ranks in the restaurant world in what is sometimes called the "French brigade system." The position titles are as follows:

Commis Chef—An apprentice chef, tasked with cleaning the kitchen as well as scrubbing and peeling vegetables. The average salary for this position is $20,000 a year.

Chef de Partie—After learning all areas of the kitchen, the apprentice chef is promoted to chef de partie, also known as a line cook. At this level, the chef has one specific task to do, such as deep frying foods, making pastries, or cooking fish. The usual salary is around $30,000 a year.

Sous Chef—Also known as the assistant chef, the sous chef is second in command. The sous chef helps make schedules, works with customers, and fills in for the executive chef when needed. The salary averages around $40,000 a year.

Executive Chef—The highest level, the executive chef is in complete charge of the kitchen. He or she is responsible for planning menus, creating new recipes, planning the budget, managing the staff, and supervising food preparations. A typical salary would be around $70,000, but top chefs can earn much more.

In 1988 Ramsay was working in 27-year-old Marco Pierre White's kitchen when Marco became the youngest chef in Britain to earn two Michelin stars.

slapped and kicked and punched. And when the chef shouted at me, I listened, took it in and said, "Oui, chef". . . . At Harvey's, I took the flak till the cows came home. Marco pushed me as far as possible; it was a test of strength and yes we went to the limit and yes I know it was worth it."

After three years at Harvey's Ramsay was capable of running White's kitchen by himself. But in 1988 the two men had a falling out. Marco had ordered Gordon to evict his roommate, a fellow chef whom Marco had just fired. Ramsay refused, and was fired as well. Although White later rehired Gordon, the incident inspired him to strike off on his own.

LE GAVROCHE

Ramsay went to work for White's first London employers, Albert and Michel Roux. The two brothers from France ran Le Gavroche, a restaurant in Mayfair, an area in central London. They were renowned cooks, who said they were bringing French cuisine to England in order to turn "a nation of culinary barbarians into one of gourmets." (English food had long been mocked as being of low quality.)

Albert and Michel were strict taskmasters with high standards. And Gordon gave them his best effort during the 18 months he worked for them. But they encouraged him to learn more about classic French cuisine in the country where it originated. So in the fall of 1989, he left to further his training in Paris.

GUY SAVOY

Living in Paris was an adjustment for 23-year-old Ramsay, as he didn't know the French language very well. He worked at Guy Savoy, a restaurant named for and run by one of France's top chefs. Not fully understanding the French language proved a benefit, however, as Savoy frequently yelled at Gordon in French. But Ramsay didn't take the insults personally. "You're in a house that's phenomenal," he later explained. "Who the hell am I to walk in there and think I shouldn't be upset when they tell me off?" He added, "There's a lot of determination and frustration and aggression that goes into making something perfect, and there's a price to pay for it."

Among the many lessons Ramsay learned was the importance of not wasting food. "In Paris, I learned total respect for food, and how cleverly you can make something out of nothing," he explained. "Take a leek. At Harvey's we would take a forty-inch leek and use about half of it—half an inch of white stuff to finish a soup or to use as a garnish. The rest of it would be binned. In France, you'd use the best white bit for the soup, but then you'd use the rest for a sauce, the top of it for a mousse, and then the very top of it, you'd use in a staff meal. Nothing went in the bin."

Gordon also learned the importance of quality in selecting ingredients, because the finest ingredients guarantee the taste of a quality dish. "One of the many things Guy taught me is that flavour is the most important aspect of a dish," he later said. "I trained my palate in Paris and learned that taste is what should be held in the memory, not what the dish looks like on the plate for the first 30 seconds. People pay big money for food which tastes phenomenal, not just for something which looks pretty when it gets to your table."

Apprentices are paid only a minimum wage in France. Gordon's apprentice salary was so meager that he had to take another part-time job in a coffee shop. But he did make some money by winning a competition back in London. His former bosses, the Roux brothers, had signed him up for a National Chef of the Year competition in London, and Ramsay had made it to the semifinals. He traveled back for the cooking contest and with his specialties of risotto, ravioli of lobster, and crème brulee with a jus Granny Smith, took home some prize money.

JAMIN

The following year, Gordon trained with Joel Robuchon, a Michelin star French chef whose restaurant, Jamin, was considered the most famous in the world. "Robuchon was such an unpleasant person to work for," Ramsay would later say. "To the French public, he portrayed himself as cool and sophisticated, the real deal. But in the kitchen, he was just a tyrant. If he threw a plate at you, you weren't to expect an apology. The next day, he wouldn't even say 'good morning' to you."

Designated in 1989 as "Chef of the Century," Joel Robuchon later built an international restaurant empire. In 2010 he earned his 26th Michelin star.

MICHELIN STARS

The Michelin star rating system originated in 1900, when two brothers in France first published the Michelin guides. Andre and Edouard Michelin owned a tire factory at a time when automobiles were still a novelty. They produced guidebooks to help new travelers find places to get fuel for their cars and locate decent places to eat on their journeys. The purpose of the books was to encourage people to get out and drive more.

During the 1920s, the Michelin Company established a star rating system to evaluate the restaurants listed in the guide. Inspectors were sent to rate dining establishments according to certain criteria such as taste, freshness of the ingredients, originality of the food, and the restaurant's atmosphere. As of 1931 highly rated restaurants received one to three stars according to the following system:

One star: "a very good restaurant in its own category"
Two stars: "excellent cooking, worth a detour"
Three stars: "exceptional cuisine, worth a special trip"

Anonymous, professionally trained experts pretending to be regular customers evaluate a restaurant's food and service. They visit a place three or four times before giving it a star. More than 240 restaurants are inspected each year. The ratings are published in the *Michelin Red Guide*, which is printed on a yearly basis. Today, fewer than 100 restaurants worldwide receive three Michelin stars.

But Ramsay stayed. "I wanted to learn from this guy," he later said. "He was the best chef in the world." Ramsay lasted 10 months working under the volatile chef. He continued to improve his understanding of classic French cooking, as well as his mastery of the French language.

Ramsay has recognized the value of his culinary training in Paris. He says, "The two and half years I had in France were the most important years of my life. . . . I built some fantastic foundations for my future in those years."

Personal Chef

But the 18-hour days were taking their toll. Despite the long hours Ramsay was spending in Paris's finest restaurant kitchens, he was not making enough to pay his bills. And he was far from having enough money to open up his own restaurant. So when the opportunity arose to leave behind the hectic hours of a high-pressure fine-dining restaurant and work as a personal chef, he took it.

In 1992 Gordon accepted a commission to work on a yacht owned by Reg Grundy, an Australian television magnate, and his wife, Joy Chambers. The job paid well; Ramsay received a hefty salary of £4,000 (around $6,500) a month. And he did not always have to work since the Grundys used the yacht only about three months of the year. When the owners and their friends were on board, Ramsay had plenty to do. He adapted his French cuisine to meet Reg Grundy's needs for a low-fat diet, at the same time developing a signature style of gourmet fare.

When the media mogul and his wife were not on board, Ramsay could spend his time as he wished. He typically fished, went scuba diving or running, and mingled with the other crewmembers.

His stint as a personal chef brought Gordon much needed rest, but after nine months he found himself growing restless. To reach his goal of opening his own place, he would have to end his life of leisure. "I kept my imaginary restaurant—my dream—in my mind's eye at all times." Gordon recalled later. "I never let myself forget that this, for me, was just another leg in my journey."

BACK IN LONDON

In 1993 Ramsay was back in London. Upon his return to the city, he was approached by Pierre Koffman, the owner of La Tante Claire, a three-star restaurant in the Chelsea section of London. Koffman's cook had just quit, and he offered Ramsay the position of head chef. Gordon had saved £15,000 (around $22,500) from his work as a yacht chef, but that was not enough money to set up his own restaurant. So he accepted the position at La Tante Claire.

However, Ramsay did not stay long in the position. He later said that he sensed a rivalry with Koffman, who would not allow Gordon to list many of his specialties on the menu. After only three months at La Tante Claire, he was willing to listen to another offer.

AUBERGINE

It was around this time that Ramsay got a phone call from Marco Pierre White. Gordon's former boss wanted to introduce him to three Italian bankers who had started up a company called A to Z Restaurants, Ltd. The company had purchased The Rossmore, a failing restaurant in Chelsea, and was in desperate need of an executive chef who could turn things around. White had suggested Ramsay, and A to Z offered Gordon a 10 percent share in the restaurant under the condition that Ramsay move fast. The plan was to close the place down and reopen it in just one week.

Ramsay accepted the challenge. He hired staff and had the space redecorated. When he chose a name for the new restaurant, he settled on one that evoked vibrancy and health—aubergine was not only his favorite color, a dark shade of purple, but it also a vegetable. In England, it is another word for "eggplant."

Aubergine opened on October 10, 1993, and was an immediate success. Its excellent food brought in numerous customers, who raved about Ramsay's specialties and light sauces, which used less butter and cream than those found in classic French cuisine. The dishes were simple, rather than elaborate and included foods such as fish poached in red wine, a consommé flavored with Earl Grey tea, and roasted shellfish served with ginger cream. Haute cuisine foods like truffles, caviar, and foie gras were also in abundance. Ramsay designed a different menu for each season.

At Aubergine Ramsay also gained a reputation as a temperamental chef. "He was an animal, a monster; he was horrible," Ramsay protégé Angela Hartnett said of her boss's behavior at that time. "He'd always say, 'Why are you diluting my standards?'" She began working in the Aubergine kitchen in 1994 and recalled that "[Ramsay] was there at seven in the morning, and he was still grafting away until one the next morning . . . . He was just really driven. And slightly mad. You were going into this crazy environment where everyone was screaming and shouting." She has said that she had oysters thrown at her by Ramsay, who insisted she'd opened them imperfectly.

Eighteen-hour days were typical, with Gordon often arriving in the early morning to tend to bookkeeping and to check the menu and food. He kept expenses low, paying himself a salary of only £22,000 (around $33,000). The restaurant quickly became popular, and tables at the celebrity hotspot soon had to be reserved months in advance.

In January 1995 Aubergine received a Michelin star. However, Ramsay's competitive nature would not allow him to celebrate, he told an interviewer. "Minutes later, I found out that Marco won three. Do you know how depressing that was?"

The food served at Aubergine inspired Gordon's first published cookbook. *Passion for Flavour*, which came out in the fall of 1996, featured 100 recipes that ranged from appetizers, to main dishes, to desserts. It included recipes of some of the dishes he served at Aubergine, and was presented in a format that could easily be followed by nonprofessional chefs.

"A NICE RELATIONSHIP"

Despite the commitment of running a new restaurant, Gordon still made time for his personal life. He frequently spent free time with his friend and fellow chef Tim Powell, who was engaged to a young woman, 18-year-old Cayetana Elizabeth Hutcheson. Tana, as she was known, was studying to be a Montessori nursery school teacher. She would often join Tim and Gordon after the two men finished their work shifts. The three would unwind and talk well into the early morning hours. And in time Gordon found his feelings growing for Tana.

One evening in 1994, Gordon went to Tim and Tana's apartment to pick up the key for his motorbike, which he stored in their garage. When he saw Tana, she told him that she had broken up with Tim. That evening Gordon and Tana sat and talked for several hours. He did not leave until 5

Gordon and Tana dated for two years before deciding to marry in 1996.

o'clock in the morning. This "first date" was to be the beginning of many happy moments the two would spend together, even though it usually meant meeting around two in the morning, after Gordon finished work. It was also difficult to schedule time together as Tana worked part-time for her father and went to night school.

In the fall of 1996 Gordon asked Tana to leave her studies and part-time job for a while to vacation with him in southern France. It was then that he asked her to marry him. It was not a very romantic proposal, she noted later: "He just said, 'It's such a nice relationship. Let's get married.'" She agreed and on December, 21, 1996, Gordon, at age 29, and Tana, age 21, were married in a church in Chelsea.

The newlyweds moved into a loft apartment in an old school building in southern London, but Gordon continued to spend more hours at work than at home. Tana remained understanding of his demanding work schedule. He later said, "[S]he knew what it meant to be driven, to be obsessed with your work—she'd seen the same trait in her father. When she was growing up, he sometimes used to work twenty-four hours a day. So I never had to account for my movements to her, and I was grateful for that."

CHAPTER FOUR

GRAND OPENINGS

The year 1997 started out promising for Ramsay, as good news arrived early that year. Each January, Michelin stars are awarded to fine dining establishments around the world. The staff at Aubergine would not be disappointed, as they received word that the restaurant had received its second star.

L'ORANGER

Soon after, executives of A to Z Restaurants informed Gordon that they wanted to open a second fine-dining restaurant. They asked if he would he be able to find them a chef for the new establishment. And they offered him a 10 percent share of the new restaurant.

Gordon immediately thought of his friend and protégé, Marcus Wareing, who had been working as a sous chef at Aubergine since its opening in 1993. Ramsay and Wareing had first met when both worked in the kitchen of Le Gavroche; Marcus at the time was a 19-year-old trainee chef.

A to Z hired Wareing as head chef of the new restaurant with the understanding that Ramsay would supervise.

In the summer of 1997, L'Oranger opened its doors on St. James Street, in London. Within six months, it received its first Michelin star.

NO CLONES

With its two restaurants doing so well, executives at A to Z Restaurants wanted to expand. In early 1998 they approached Ramsay with a plan to build duplicate Aubergines all over the world. There would be an Aubergine Paris, Aubergine New York, and Aubergine Bermuda. They also considered opening small cafes and bistros as well. And they insisted that Ramsay and Wareing sign multiyear contracts with the company.

Gordon did not like the idea of a restaurant chain, of starting up restaurants that were exactly alike. "I would have had to replicate everything at Aubergine as a concept in catering," he explained. "But restaurants of this nature are personal, not concept. My choice was to be an individual. I don't want to produce clones."

And neither Ramsay nor Waering wanted to commit to long-term contracts with A to Z either. Gordon was in a difficult situation. The contract he was being asked to sign limited his ability to open up his own restaurant; it stated that he couldn't launch another dining establishment within 25 miles of Aubergine. He also knew that the two restaurants could be sold out from under him. He had been given a 10 percent share in A to Z, but that small stake meant he had little say in the decision-making. In addition, he worried that the other restaurant shareholders were looking to Marco Pierre White to replace him at Aubergine.

A Selection of Gourmet Foods

beignet—a fritter or square of fried dough sprinkled with confectioners sugar.

black pudding—blood sausage.

celeriac—a variety of celery shaped like a turnip root .

Colston Bassett—a special English cheese made with blue mold spores.

confit—duck or other meat cooked slowly in its own fat.

daikon—a mild, very large, white East Asian radish.

langoustine—a small lobster with thin claws.

leek—a vegetable in the onion family that has a white bulb and tall flat leaves.

morel—an edible mushroom with a brown oval or pointed body and an irregular, ridged surface.

pate de foie gras—a smooth paste made from the liver of a duck or goose that has been force-fed corn.

pommes boulangere—a potato dish containing thinly sliced potatoes, garlic, onions and herbs.

porcini—Italian for "little pigs," this large brown capped wild mushroom has a mild, nutty flavor and smooth texture.

risotto—an Italian dish made with rice cooked in a broth, and often including meat, cheese and vegetables.

sweetbreads—the glands of an animal such as the throat, gullet, pancreas, and thymus.

tagliatelle—long, flat pieces of egg noodles.

tarte tatin—a kind of upside-down pie with carmelized fruit.

truffle—a fungus delicacy that can cost up to $2,400 per pound, truffles look like small, rough-skinned potatoes, ranging in size from a dime to a large golf ball.

In early spring someone on a moped pulled up in front of Aubergine and made a mad dash inside to the restaurant's foyer. He grabbed the reservation book and took off with it. The theft of the book created chaos at the restaurant. Because the kitchen staff had no idea how many people were scheduled for dinners or what days and times were open for new customers, it was difficult to determine how much food to purchase.

In the months that followed the thief would regularly fax the restaurant the previous night's reservation page, which by then was of little use to the staff. Despite the anonymous taunting faxes, the police were unable to discover the culprit or find the missing book. However, Aubergine managed to remain in business. (In 2007 Ramsay would admit that he was behind the theft. Worried that White wanted to take over his position at the restaurant, he arranged to have the book stolen to make the A to Z shareholders suspicious of White. And he had succeeded. After the theft, the shareholders cut White off.)

RESTAURANT GORDON RAMSAY

Ramsay was considering all his options. One was an offer by David Levin, the owner of The Greenhouse, a restaurant in the Mayfair section of London. Levin had offered Ramsay a yearly salary of £150,000 (about $250,000), plus 5 percent of the business if he would accept the position of head chef at the restaurant. But during the negotiations with Levin, Ramsay realized that what he really wanted to do was to open his own restaurant. It was time for him to try to follow his dream.

Tana's father, Chris Hutcheson, a businessman who owned a printing company, advised Gordon during The

Greenhouse negotiations. At that time he encouraged Ramsay to open his own place, and he soon helped his son-in-law secure a loan from the Bank of Scotland for £2 million (around $3 million). Gordon and Chris each held a 50 percent share in the new dining establishment, and they formed a business partnership called Gordon Ramsay Holdings, Limited. Ramsay would run the restaurant kitchen, while Hutcheson would be responsible for the restaurant business operations.

At the beginning of August, A to Z executives renewed their efforts to have Ramsay and Wareing sign long-term contracts. As a shareholder in the company, Gordon had to accompany Giuliano Lotto, the head of A to Z Restaurants, when he went to L'Oranger to tell Marcus to sign or be fired. When Marcus refused, he was told to leave.

Gordon would later say that he called the restaurant staff together, told the workers what had happened, and announced that in support of Marcus, he was quitting, too. He also informed the staff that he was in the process of opening his own restaurant. "You're more than welcome to come and join me," he stated. "I hope there'll be a job there for all of you, but at the moment, nothing is certain. I'm leaving because I'm not happy with the direction this business is going in. If you want to hand in your notice and follow me, that's up to you." According to Ramsay, the entire group—all 46 employees—showed their loyalty. They immediately stopped everything they were doing, gathered up their belongings, and walked out with him.

A to Z Restaurants was left with two restaurants that had no chefs and no staff. Reservations at Aubergine and L'Oranger had to be canceled, and new workers interviewed and hired. During the time they had to shut down to reorgan-

Gordon shouts instructions while cooking at Restaurant Gordon Ramsay, in the Chelsea district of London, circa 1998.

ize, the shareholders lost a great deal of money. They sued Ramsay for more than $1.5 million. The suit would be settled out of court in 2000 for an unspecified amount.

Since Ramsay had already begun setting up his first independently owned venture, he was able to open his new restaurant quickly. In early September 1998, five weeks after leaving Aubergine, Restaurant Gordon Ramsay, on Royal Hospital Road in Chelsea, opened its doors. That first night did not go smoothly. "We had 52 people in the restaurant and the air conditioning went down in the kitchen," Gordon explained. "I just couldn't afford to close. So we had to cook in temperatures of 150 degrees . . . It was absolutely horrendous, one of the worst nights of my entire life."

But the effort proved worthwhile as the new restaurant was an early success. It soon became famous for Ramsay's signature dishes such as lobster ravioli in a lemon grass and chervil sauce, and cappuccino of white beans with grated white truffles.

CONTROVERSY

Soon after Restaurant Gordon Ramsay opened, Gordon found himself at the center of controversy. He had previously had a run-in with *Sunday Times* restaurant critic A. A. Gill. When Gill had reviewed Aubergine in 1996, he described Ramsay as a "failed sportsman." This had bothered Gordon, who told Gill that he should focus on critiquing the food and not make personal attacks.

Two years later, Gill made reservations at Gordon's new restaurant under a different name. On October 12, he showed up with his girlfriend and the actress Joan Collins. After they ordered but before being served, Gill and his friends were spotted by Ramsay. The chef came out of the kitchen, quietly approached the table, shook Gill's hand, and asked his party to leave, which they did. The newspapers ran with the story that not only had A. A. Gill been thrown out of Ramsay's restaurant, but also renowned actress Joan Collins.

Ramsay was 31 in 1998, when he opened Restaurant Gordon Ramsay, in Chelsea, London. It was awarded three Michelin stars within three years of opening.

Gordon responded he was acting in support of his staff. He insisted that Gill had insulted the waiter. "People said I threw him out for the publicity. Utter crap," he insisted. "I'm protective of my family and my staff. If it was the food he was complaining about, I would take it on the chin. . . . I don't mind if people criticise food, or even call me a failed footballer. But over the past two or three years he's become personal and vindictive."

UNFINISHED BUSINESS

Meanwhile, life was also busy at home. In late 1998 Tana and Gordon welcomed a daughter, Megan Jane. Right around the same time, he received a call from his father. It had been more than a decade since the two had spoken. Gordon's mother had remarried. But her former husband had continued to have little luck with life or his battle with alcoholism.

Gordon's father was living in Margate in Kent, around 75 miles from London. He would be in the city for a doctor's appointment, he told his son, and the two arranged to meet. As they spoke for a while, Gordon slowly began to feel reconciled with his father. "It was as if we had resolved something that day," he said later. The two men arranged to meet again the following month so that Gordon's father could meet Tana and Megan and then join Gordon for a meal at his restaurant.

Truffles grow three to four inches beneath the surface in certain kinds of soils that are found especially in France. Dogs and pigs—animals that have a strong sense of smell—are trained to help find this expensive delicacy hidden in the ground.

Sadly, that meeting never took place. Around 3:30 in the morning of December 31 Ramsay's phone rang. On the other end of the line, a woman was screaming about someone named Ricky Scott. Gordon didn't recognize the name and hung up. Then he wondered whether she was calling about his father. He called the woman back and found out that his father, who had changed his name, had suffered a massive heart attack. He died within 24 hours. Gordon later commented,

> No one should die at just 53. I am so angry at him for dying so young and for not looking after himself. And I couldn't believe I would never now get the fatherly seal of approval I so longed for. I had managed to have that one frank talk with him in Margate before he died. But I really wanted to ask him much more. Was he relieved about what I had done? Was he proud? I never got the chance. I got the feeling of unfinished business that will probably be with me for the rest of my life.

On January 25, 1999, the day he had planned to serve his father a dinner in his own place, Gordon set a table for two in the restaurant, in memory of his dad. Years later, he summed up his thoughts about his father in an interview with *Times Online*, "My father taught me a lot; everything he did I've done the opposite."

BOILING POINT

Gordon's father did not live long enough to see his son attain television celebrity in Great Britain. That occurred the following February when a documentary about his high-pressure kitchen aired. Before leaving Aubergine, Ramsay had agreed to being filmed for a documentary about what goes on

Gordon poses proudly with members of his kitchen staff shortly after learning that Restaurant Gordon Ramsay had been awarded three stars in the 2001 Michelin Guide. Although TV programs often depict the chef shouting angrily at his underlings in the kitchen, many cooks who have worked with Gordon say they are not bothered by his strong language and antics.

in a professional kitchen. So television cameras were rolling during the weeks that he set up his new restaurant and then in the months that followed as he worked hard to earn a Michelin star rating for it. The documentary, called *Boiling Point*, aired on Channel 4 as a five-part miniseries.

In each episode, viewers got an up close and personal look at Ramsay's kitchen. They watched in fascination and horror as the executive chef screamed and cursed at his workers. Gordon bellowed with anger when a cook ran out of salad. He threw a tray of soups into the sink when another cook brought it out at the wrong time. When a waiter stopped to take a sip from a water bottle, Ramsay immediately fired him for drinking in view of the customers. Many viewers were appalled by how Gordon treated his staff—using personal jabs to insult their cooking, calling them names, and even throwing food at them.

The Independent Television Commission, an organization that monitors TV programs in the United Kingdom, received hundreds of complaints about Ramsay's treatment of his workers and swearing. Channel 4 was asked to bleep out the strong language, but it happened so often that censors couldn't keep up. In response, ITV Studios, which produced the show, included a warning for viewers at the beginning of each subsequent episode about potentially offensive content.

The show produced strong reactions—people either loved Ramsay for his enthusiasm or hated him for his abusive manner. Numerous television reviewers discussed the controversial young chef and the show. Some complained that *Boiling Point* was causing students to turn away from the cooking industry, while others hailed Ramsay for his passion for cooking.

"I WILL NEVER APOLOGISE"

Gordon has often defended the need to swear in the kitchen. "All I am using is the language you hear in every kitchen," he has explained. "Everyone swears in kitchens if they want to produce the best food. If a kitchen is silent and everyone says 'please' and 'thank you', then you'd never hit the heights. I'm focused on producing the best and, if swearing makes that happen then I'll keep doing it."

And Gordon has said there was no reason to stop: "I'm doing it for a specific reason, to get the very best results and create the very best food. I'm a different man inside and outside of the kitchen and I will never apologise for that."

By 2004, Gordon and Tana's family had grown to four children: Megan (born 1998), twins Jack and Holly (born 2000), and Matilda (born 2002).

CHAPTER FIVE

FAMILY, FRIENDS, AND PARTNERSHIPS

In order to spend time with Tana and his family, Gordon chose for many years not to open his restaurant on weekends, even though the practice meant losing money. He and Tana also made an effort to carve out dates in their hectic schedules so they could spend time together. But telephones continued to be their main method of communication. They would talk to each other on the phone several times a day.

The Ramsays' busy lifestyle became even more complicated in 1999. That is when Gordon branched out and opened another restaurant.

PETRUS

Gordon Ramsay Holdings launched the new restaurant, which Ramsay opened with Marcus Wareing, who also served as executive chef. They called the restaurant Petrus, which was the name of Marcus's favorite wine. The fine dining establishment opened on St. James Street, in London, although in 2003 it would move to the Berkeley Hotel.

47

Petrus attracted an immediate flurry of customers. Its popularity resulted from the high quality of its food, as evident by its receipt of a Michelin star within seven months of opening. "Ramsay's food is vibrant, the flavour of the moment and is executed to the very highest level," raved the Michelin judge. "Gordon Ramsay can no longer be ignored."

NEW YEAR SURPRISE

The Michelin star for Petrus in January 2000 had been preceded by another happy event in the Ramsay household. In 1999 Tana became pregnant with twins, who were due in February 2000. To welcome in the New Year she and Gordon invited more than 100 friends and family to a private New Year's Eve party at Restaurant Gordon Ramsay.

On the day of December 31, Gordon was in the restaurant kitchen preparing for the party. He was cooking feverishly, as most of his staff had the day off. In the midst of chopping and dicing, Gordon received a phone call from Tana. She told him that she was not feeling well and that she might be having contractions. The twins weren't due for another five weeks, so Gordon didn't take her seriously. He suggested that she rest a bit, and he kept on working.

Two hours later, the phone rang again. It was Tana calling to tell him she was being "taken down." Gordon was confused

In a story reported in London newspapers, six London bankers spent $63,000 on dinner at Petrus. After they tried to have their company pay for the meal as a business expense, five of them were fired.

until a doctor took over the call and told him that Tana was at the hospital and was to have an emergency Caesarean section.

Frantic with worry, Gordon ran out of the restaurant and tried to hail a taxi. But it was New Year's Eve, and he couldn't find one. So he set off on foot, planning to run the four miles to the hospital. Fortunately, after going only a short distance, he managed to find a cab. But by the time he finally arrived at the hospital, his new son and daughter, Jack Scott and Holly Anna, had already been born.

More Cookbooks

Ramsay's second cookbook, *Passion for Seafood*, had been published in 1999. He followed it with a third cookbook in 2000. *A Chef for All Seasons* boasted more than 100 easy recipes full of fresh ingredients. Some of the unusual offerings include "Cherry Soup with Caramel-Balsamic Ice" and "Summer Lobster with Mango and Spinach Salad."

In 2001 Gordon produced *Gordon Ramsay's Just Desserts*. This book included recipes with complex tastes and elegant presentations such as "Steamed Toffee, Banana, and Pecan Pudding," "Chocolate Mocha Tart," and "Fresh Lavender Ice Cream."

Amaryllis

Gordon Ramsay Holdings opened a third restaurant in April 2001. This one had a special significance for Gordon, as it was located in Scotland.

Ramsay hired his friend and protégé David Dempsey to serve as executive chef of the new place, called Amaryllis, in Glasgow. Gordon had known David, a fellow Scotsman, since 1998. He had worked as a junior sous chef at Restaurant Gordon Ramsay before being asked to take on the role of head chef of the new venture in the city they both considered home.

CLARIDGE'S

Soon after, the private-equity firm Blackstone Group LP asked Ramsay to run a restaurant in one of the four hotels it then owned in London. Claridge's, in Mayfair, was a historic and very prestigious five-star hotel. Since the 1850s, the legendary place had been patronized by guests such as Queen Victoria, British prime ministers Winston Churchill and Margaret Thatcher, and U.S. first lady Nancy Reagan.

Gordon Ramsay at Claridge's opened in the fall of 2001. As executive chef, Gordon held total charge of the restaurant. At the same time he continued as head chef at Restaurant Gordon Ramsay, in Chelsea, which had received its third Michelin star that year and been voted the top restaurant in the U.K. in the 2001 London Zagat survey.

Ramsay explained that he could serve as executive chef at both restaurants because they were located so close together. He had clocked the drive between the restaurant in Chelsea and the one in Mayfair at seven and a half minutes, and he would zip back and forth between the two places to supervise and direct.

The new restaurant was an immediate hit, and Ramsay was quick to promote its popularity. A couple of weeks after Gordon Ramsay at Claridge's opened, an ad appeared in the

The Chelsea and Mayfair neighborhoods are both located in central London. Many expensive residential properties are found in Chelsea, while Mayfair is home to many of the city's luxury hotels and restaurants.

Gordon and his protégé Marcus Wareing in the dining room of Gordon Ramsay at Claridges, 2001. The two chefs worked together at several award-winning restaurants, including Petrus and the Savoy Grill.

London newspaper the *Daily Mail*. Gordon wrote the notice, which described how the staff in charge of reservation bookings was being overwhelmed:

> A monster has arrived in London's posh Mayfair. It wasn't there two weeks ago, but it has roared in on a whirlwind of culinary interest and curiosity. Yes, it's my Gordon Ramsay at Claridge's restaurant. It is generating a hurricane of activity. Yesterday we received more than 500 telephone calls for reservations. And 300 faxes. The response has been phenomenal and, in only the second week, we have welcomed 1,500 clients. . . . Booking is open from 8am to 10pm—and there are four telephonists trying to secure the breach every time a fresh wave crashes through.

Interest in Claridge's would remain strong, and Ramsay's reputation continued to grow. Many restaurant customers wanted to see Gordon while he worked. So in the spring of 2002, he set up a "chef's table" in the kitchen of Claridge's for customers willing to pay extra for a behind-the-scenes view. At the chef's table, a party can sit and watch the excitement in the kitchen from behind a glass wall that surrounds them on three sides.

MORE HOTEL RESTAURANTS

The year 2001 saw Ramsay open up his first international restaurant. Verre is in the Dubai Hilton Creek Hotel, in the city of Dubai, which is located in the United Arab Emirates. It featured a modern European menu in an elegant, but simple setting.

Gordon's company was back to focusing on London restaurants in 2002, when Blackstone Group put Ramsay in charge of the food and beverage areas in the Connaught Hotel, located in Mayfair. Le Menu at the Connaught was headed by Angela Hartnett, who was the first woman to serve as an executive chef in a London five star hotel.

The following year the Blackstone Group also had Ramsay running The Savoy Grill. Located in the Savoy Hotel, the distinguished eatery opened under the direction of Marcus Wareing. The year 2003 also saw Ramsay launch the Boxwood Cafe under the direction of Stuart Gillies; it was located in the Blackstone-owned Berkeley Hotel.

The new restaurants featured quality food that would earn them honors and awards. In 2003 Gordon Ramsay at Claridge's received its first Michelin star. The Savoy Grill earned its Michelin star in January 2004.

Another Gordon Ramsay protégé, Angela Hartnett (left) works in the kitchen at Le Menu at The Connaught in London. Hartnett had worked with Marcus Wareing and Gordon at Aubergine and Petrus, and helped David Dempsey launch Amaryllis in Scotland. Le Menu at the Connaught won a "Best New Restaurant" award from a London food guide in 2003; the next year, Hartnett received her first Michelin star.

A NEW HOME

Amid the flurry and success of new businesses, there was also excitement at home, as the Ramsays welcomed their fourth child, Matilda Elizabeth. Tilly, as she was nicknamed, was born in 2002.

To accommodate their growing family, Gordon and Tana purchased a three-story Victorian home in South London. The building had been partitioned into four separate apartments, and after settling on the house, Gordon and Tana converted the apartments into a huge family home, complete with 10 bedrooms.

Included in the major renovation was the installation of a 2.5 ton Rorgue stove, which had to be lowered by a crane into the kitchen. This stove, which is about the size of a car, cost approximately $109,000. A second cooking area was built in the lower level, but Tana has insisted that the larger room with the Rorgue stove is not just Gordon's kitchen, but the family kitchen.

In the early 2000s, Gordon found himself constantly on the move as he managed restaurants throughout the United Kingdom as well as in the United Arab Emirates.

A SUDDEN TRAGEDY

Within a year of its opening in 2001, Amaryllis in Glasgow had earned a Michelin star. So in February 2003 Gordon promoted David Dempsey, who was in charge of Amaryllis, by appointing him to the position of head chef at Restaurant Gordon Ramsay in Chelsea.

Gordon did not know that 31-year-old David had been struggling with money problems and worries that an illness he had battled once before, Hodgkin's disease, was resurfacing. At the same time, Dempsey was having trouble dealing with staff at his new job. Soon after he arrived at Restaurant Gordon Ramsay, three chefs quit.

On May 3 Ramsay had a dinner meeting with Dempsey to discuss the staff issues and to suggest alternative methods of management. Gordon would later say that he thought that the meeting went well. But, he noted that Dempsey did not seem himself. "He was not 100% David. He was slightly agitated—a guy that for me was looking as if he was under pressure," he said.

The next night, that pressure ended in tragedy. On May 4, 2003, around 11 P.M., Dempsey climbed the scaffolding at the rear of a four-story complex in Chelsea, entered an empty apartment, and began breaking windows. A frightened resident in the complex tried to fight him off using a golf club, but Dempsey grabbed the club and used it to smash more windows. He then climbed outside, and began to move from window ledge to window ledge. He was 40 feet high when he lost his grip and fell. He died from a broken neck and severe injuries to his head and back.

Dempsey's bizarre behavior was later attributed to alcohol and cocaine use, which caused a cocaine delirium and a drug-fueled rampage. The coroner found that Dempsey had

DEALING WITH A HIGH-PRESSURE JOB

A chef in a high-end restaurant normally works a 14-hour day, typically beginning around 9 A.M. and working until after midnight. His or her responsibilities include planning food supplies, filling gaps in staff, and supervising staff as they work in the kitchen. In order to stay awake and energetic during long days, some kitchen chefs have been known to use stimulants that they have obtained either legally or illegally.

Ramsay discounts the idea that a person needs drugs to work in a professional kitchen, and he adamantly states that he does not use them himself. "People say you need drugs to provide the energy for this job. It's the biggest load of rubbish," he insists. "The pressure does not drive anyone to having a dependency on chemicals. It does not drive anyone to taking coke. I'm sure there are drugs in the industry. But I don't smoke, I don't drink. I go to the gym three days a week and I run 40 miles. When I see young guys coming into my kitchen, I do fear for them but I say to them all, 'If you're not here to enjoy it later in life, what's the point?'

Gordon credits regular exercise with helping him deal with the high stress of the restaurant business. Here, he competes in a 2009 marathon in London.

taken a potentially fatal amount of cocaine. On May 8 Gordon traveled to Scotland to break the news to the staff at Amaryllis in Glasgow. There, he noted, "I am completely shocked and devastated. David has worked for me for the past eight years and was not only a brilliant protégé but also a friend."

Gordon would later say that he saw no signs that Dempsey was using drugs. If he had been, he would have been fired. Ramsay has affirmed, "We have zero tolerance of drugs and they do not enter any professional kitchen that we run. Anyone found taking any form of illegal substance would be immediately sacked."

CLOSING DOWN

After David Dempsey's death, Ramsay had to make a decisions about whether to keep Amaryllis going. Although the place would be packed on weekends, it was empty during the workweek, and was losing money. In a way, shutting down Amaryllis, as difficult as it was to do, helped bring some closure to Ramsay's memories of David. The restaurant was shuttered in early 2004.

Another restaurant that Gordon was involved with also closed in January 2004. The reason given was that the Fleur, located in London, was not for economic reasons, but due to a conflict over the leasing agreement on the building.

Despite these closings, Gordon Ramsay Holdings was still worth millions. As of February 2005, it had launched seven restaurants in London. And Ramsay's flagship restaurant—his first dining establishment, Restaurant Gordon Ramsay—had been a three Michelin star restaurant since 2001.

In 2005, the Fox network hired Gordon to host a reality television show for American audiences, making him an international celebrity.

CHAPTER SIX

TV CELEBRITY

Many people outside the fine dining world, including television producers, noticed Gordon after *Boiling Point* aired in the U.K. in 1999. It was quickly followed by a six-part documentary called *Beyond Boiling Point*, which Channel 4 broadcast in 2000. The film shows Ramsay's efforts in trying to obtain Michelin star ratings for his restaurants. With his newfound celebrity, Gordon soon received many invitations to appear on other shows.

FRIENDS FOR DINNER

In July 2001 Gordon was on *Friends for Dinner*, broadcast on BBC. The show paired top chefs with ordinary people, with the idea that each chef would help his or her partner put together a gourmet dinner. This meant planning the menu, providing copies of cookbooks, and giving tips in the kitchen. One of the stipulations was that while the dinner party was in progress, the contestant could call the chef to ask for tips and advice.

Gordon was assigned to help a 40-year-old management consultant named Simon Law. But the two did not get along.

Gordon asked him to come to his restaurant for a couple of days of training. "I thought it would be a nice gesture to have him in my kitchen," he later said, "but it was two days of hell. He has not been told he is wrong in 30 years, he wasn't interested in learning and he was rude."

The cameras were filming a few days later when Simon called Gordon at the restaurant while he was in the middle of a busy lunch hour. Ramsay, who was under pressure to get food out to his customers, cut the call short by smashing the phone against a wall and pitching it in the trash. Still later, the two men got involved in a powdered sugar fight in the restaurant kitchen. The clashes in personality made for good reality television. Simon Law held no grudges, later commenting, "[H]e may be a vicious git in the kitchen, but away from all that, Gordon is actually a very nice guy."

FAKING IT

That year Ramsay also appeared on the Channel 4 reality program *Faking It*. The purpose of the show was for contestants to learn how be pretend to be something they were not—and to successfully fool the program's judges. In Ramsay's case, he had to take someone with a minimum of cooking skills and train that person to appear as if he were a head chef of a fine dining establishment. Gordon, with the help of sev-

The *Faking It* episode titled "Burger Flipper To Chef," which featured Gordon training Ed Devlin as a chef, aired on November 6, 2001. It would win a British Academy of Film and Television Arts (BAFTA) award for Best Factual TV Moment of 2001.

eral other chefs, had four weeks to teach the trade to a timid short-order cook named Ed Devlin.

Ed's first efforts were disasters, but with time his cooking, as well as his chopping and dicing skills, began to improve. He was beginning to look like a convincing head chef in all but one area—the mild mannered man had trouble taking charge. He hated yelling and screaming, and disliked telling others what to do. When, as part of the program, he worked in Gordon's restaurant kitchen, he was shocked that Gordon not only bellowed and swore at his employees, but also at him.

Gordon's solution to teaching Ed some decision-making and leadership skills was to make him serve as referee in a game of soccer. When Ed saw the similarities between taking charge in the kitchen and taking charge in a game, something clicked. When the day of the competition arrived, Ed was able to orchestrate his team into preparing an exquisite three-course dinner of red mullet for 12 people. All three program judges assumed Devlin had to be a real chef, which won him the show for "faking it."

Ed appreciated the help he got from Gordon, and like Simon Law had positive things to say about Ramsay: "Gordon is actually a very likeable guy and I won't have a bad word said against him," said Devlin. "He is inspiring to be around and once he steps inside the kitchen he changes and comes alive. His enthusiasm is infectious and he has this fantastic ability to raise people above the merely exceptional to verging on the sublime."

RAMSAY'S KITCHEN NIGHTMARES

Ramsay assumed full star power in 2004 when he served as host of a new reality television show in the U.K. called *Ramsay's Kitchen Nightmares*. Broadcast on Channel 4, the show had Ramsay serving as a culinary doctor, straightening out dysfunctional restaurant kitchens. Over a one-week period, he would try to make a failing establishment successful by solving its problems and even giving restaurants makeovers. He would later admit that he was shocked at how bad the food could be in some restaurants.

Ramsay shared some background about the program:

> The places we visit for *Kitchen Nightmares* are genuinely awful: dirty kitchens, with chefs who use packet sauces. . . . We've seen it all, and everything we screen is absolutely as we find it, I can promise you that. People think stuff is set up. No way. The production staff doesn't even give me any background before I get there so my reactions are all completely genuine. I never meet the restaurateurs in advance, nor do I get to read their menus. If I did, half the time I probably wouldn't bother showing up. The bottom line is, the secret of the show lies in its rawness, in its rough edges.

When *Ramsay's Kitchen Nightmares* premiered in the U.K. in April 2004, it was an immediate hit. According to polls, one out of five persons in the country watched the program. This averaged out to about 5 million viewers per week. ITV, a competitive channel in England, experienced some of its worst ratings during the *Ramsay's Kitchen Nightmares* time slot.

HELL'S KITCHEN

ITV executives invited Ramsay to host a new program to be broadcast on their network. It would be broadcast live, over a two-week period, and involve Gordon teaching a group of 10 British celebrities—all with little cooking experience—

Gordon congratulates soap-opera actress Jennifer Ellison, the winner of the first season of Hell's Kitchen *broadcast in the United Kingdom, June 2004. Gordon did not care for the show's format, because the celebrity contestants did not take their work in the kitchen seriously enough for his taste.*

how to work in a professional kitchen. A restaurant was set up in which the prepared food was to be served during the two weeks that the show ran. The reality TV cooking competition was called *Hell's Kitchen*.

The British celebrities included three actors, two singers, a comic, and a disc jockey. The aspiring chefs were divided into blue and red teams, each headed by one of Gordon's chefs, Angela Hartnett and Marcus Wareing.

The first episode of *Hell's Kitchen* was broadcast on ITV in early 2004. In his introductory speech to the contestants,

Gordon told them what he expected of them: "You will have to sweep the floor ten times an hour, peel a bucket of onions, cook for the staff. You will also scrub clean your own pans because this stops you from burning things." He added, "You'll be amazed how careful chefs are if they know they have to scrape the burned gunk off the bottom of their own saucepans." He warned them that they would find him blunt and to the point, saying, "I don't give a . . . about diplomacy or delicacy. The more honest I am with you the better you will become."

Ramsay expected a big commitment from the contestants. But they did not perform to his expectations. And as they failed to prepare acceptable dishes for the restaurant, he responded with a great deal of cursing and insults. Some contestants were reduced to tears; some of them walked out. The television ratings plummeted as many viewers stopped watching the show. The press attacked Gordon for being rude, and for pushing the contestants too far. He later explained:

> The real problem with the show was the huge gap between my expectations and that of the producers and the contestants. The producers were only worried about making a 'reality' TV programme, and the contestants were only worried about how they looked on that programme, whereas I was attempting to run a proper, fine-dining restaurant. In some sense, I felt that my reputation was on the line.

Ramsay did not film another season of *Hell's Kitchen* in the U.K. for ITV. Instead, he signed an exclusive contract with Channel 4. In 2005 he began filming a second season of *Ramsay's Kitchen Nightmares*.

THE F WORD

In 2005 Ramsay also filmed another new show for Channel 4, called *The F Word*. In the cooking magazine and food show, Ramsay hosted discussions about various aspects of food and different kinds of cuisine. *The F Word* also featured celebrity guests, cooking demonstrations, and challenges in which amateur chefs prepared meals under Ramsay's supervision.

Its first episode would air in the U.K. in October 2005. In the meantime, Gordon would be making himself familiar to U.S. television audiences.

FOX'S HELL'S KITCHEN

In the early part of 2005, BBC America had aired *Ramsay's Kitchen Nightmares* and broadcast *Boiling Point*. In late spring of that year, American audience finally got the chance to see Gordon Ramsay in the U.S. version of *Hell's Kitchen*.

The show had been changed in several ways. Instead of two weeks of live, daily shows—which was how the show was filmed and broadcast in Britain—the U.S. program was filmed over the course of six weeks and edited into one-hour episodes broadcast each week, and the series finale running two hours. The American version featured 12 contestants

In the November 2005 episode of *The F Word*, Gordon Ramsay apologized for throwing Joan Collins out of his restaurant in 1998. Collins appeared on the show and heard Ramsay say, "I'd just like to say a big apology because my mum's never forgiven me for asking you to leave. . . . You're welcome in all my restaurants any time you like."

who were ordinary members of the public, and not celebrities. In the first show, these "ordinary people" included an office assistant, a purchasing supervisor, a bartender, a finance manager, a mother of six, and some professional chefs. A former TV news studio in the Los Angeles suburb of Willoughby had been fitted out to serve as a kitchen, restaurant, and dorm area for the contestants.

Fox advertised the upcoming show with billboards promoting Ramsay's confrontational reputation: "He's world-

Gordon poses with his co-stars from the first season of Hell's Kitchen *in 2005. Mary Ann Salcedo (left) served as one of the sous chefs and team leaders for the first three seasons, while Scott Leibfried (right) has been the other sous chef for the program's entire run. Jean-Philippe Susilovic (center, back) served as maître d' on the show's first seven seasons; he held that position at Gordon's London restaurant Petrus, and also appeared on the U.K.* Hell's Kitchen.

The first episode of *Hell's Kitchen* aired in the United States on May 30, 2005. Fox celebrated the 100th episode of the program on October 13, 2010. That year *Hell's Kitchen* drew more than 6 million American viewers per episode.

renowned—and he's terrifying," the signs warned. "His show is dramatic, unscripted and he serves helpings of terror, tears, tantrums and triumphs. Ramsay will slice and dice his contestants. They will be tossed into the cauldron, working under Ramsay and fighting for survival."

In May Fox Television's version of *Hell's Kitchen*, hosted by Gordon Ramsay and produced by ITV's Los Angeles-based firm Granada America, premiered in the United States. In the first episode, each contestant faced the initial challenge of preparing a signature dish. An imperious and abusive Ramsay evaluated their efforts and bluntly told the participants his assessment of their cooking skills. Out of the twelve contestants, only two received his approval—and neither of them were experienced chefs. He disparaged the other dishes, telling one cook he had wasted 10 years of his life being a chef, and informing another that his food was pathetic.

As the nervous cooks participated in team challenges, Gordon bellowed reprimands and insults. One cook presented risotto stuck to its plate, another didn't prepare enough potatoes, and a third overcooked the fish. Gordon returned the dish by squashing it all over the man's apron.

American television audiences tuned in every week to watch the antics of the crazed British chef. By the time the two-hour final episode of season one aired in August 2005,

THE PERFECTIONIST

Gordon knows that sometimes he comes across as hard and merciless in the kitchen. In 2005, he told the *New York Times*: "I've been cooking since the age of 19, and I've never come across a namsy-wamsy, incy-pincy kitchen where everyone's a best mate. When there's no adrenaline flying high and there's very little pressure created, you don't get results."

The same article quoted chef Angela Hartnett, an executive chef in one of his restaurants. "He's a perfectionist," Hartnett said. "He demands the best, and if he has to shout to get the best, he does it. It's not like he does it every day, and in the end it's all about the food. It's constructive criticism, and it's never personal."

Ramsay insisted in the *New York Times* article that the somewhat hysterical version of himself seen on television is reinforced by the way footage is edited and that when he is not in the restaurant kitchen, he is much calmer. "I have a normal existence," he said. "I take my jacket off and leave my problems at work. You do have good days. It just doesn't show up on television."

Hell's Kitchen had the highest ratings among the 18- to 49-age group of any show featured in that time slot.

A Volatile Guy

On the downside, one of the contestants sued Ramsay after he accidentally bumped into the man, injuring his ankle. Gordon later commented, "The problem with Yanks is that they are just wimps. I've never punched anyone in a kitchen, but I have been punched." He added, "You stand there like a man, you don't wimp out and run crying for your mum. In America, they run for their attorney. I'm Gordon Ramsay, for goodness sake. People know I'm volatile. But I didn't mean to hurt the guy."

In the end, what started out as a $3 million lawsuit was settled out of court for $125,000. To a man who was worth over £20 million ($38 million) by the end of 2004, paying the money was not a major setback.

Gordon signs a copy of one of his cookbooks at a London bookstore, 2006.

CHAPTER SEVEN

A CULINARY EMPIRE

With the success of *Hell's Kitchen* in the United States, Gordon Ramsay became an international household name and celebrity television personality. But the world-renowned chef was also focusing on growing his culinary empire, as Gordon Ramsay Holdings launched new restaurants, oversaw the publishing of cookbooks, and made licensing agreements.

REVAMPING RESTAURANTS

When Ramsay's London restaurants began to receive negative reviews, critics suggested that Gordon was not properly looking after his restaurants because he was spending so much time on his television commitments.

Concerned that he would lose his hard-earned Michelin stars, Gordon revisited all his restaurants in London to see how they were faring. He saw that it was time to revamp the menus, update the food, and provide a more a relaxed atmosphere in his restaurants. He said that he wanted people from every walk of life to feel comfortable in his dining rooms. "I have always hated all that pompous . . . intimidation stuff that you used to get in every hotel restaurant in the world," he later explained. "I had to change all that in mine."

LAUNCHING NEW RESTAURANTS

As Gordon worked at developing new recipes and redesigning menus, he found that some of his more unusual foods didn't fit very well in his fine dining restaurants. This gave him the incentive to establish new restaurants that fit the food. One was an informal eatery that focused on a mix of Asian and French cuisine. Located in London at the Marriott Hotel on London's Grosvenor Square, Maze was established in 2005 with Jason Atherton as head chef.

That year Ramsay also opened another international restaurant, this one at the Conrad Tokyo Hotel in Japan. He placed one of his protégés, 28-year-old Andy Cook, at the helm of two restaurants established in the hotel.

During the press conference held to launch Gordon Ramsay at the Conrad Tokyo and Cerise by Gordon Ramsay, a reporter suggested that Ramsay was spreading himself too thin. The journalist asked who would be doing the cooking at Cerise once Gordon left Japan. Gordon answered, "The same person who is doing it when I am there." He then took a look at the reporter's Giorgio Armani suit and asked if he knew whether Giorgio had done all the stitching in the garment. Having dismissed the comment, Ramsay abruptly moved on to the next question.

MEDIA MATTERS

Gordon Ramsay Holdings not only managed all the restaurants, but it also took care of media and consultancy work. And Ramsay was taking on a lot of media work outside the kitchen—on both sides of the Atlantic. In 2005 he filmed a second series of the American program *Hell's Kitchen* in California, and a second season of *The F Word* in London.

Gordon was also producing cookbooks. In 2005 he released *Gordon Ramsay Makes It Easy*, in which he provides simple, practical recipes. (Some critics had suggested that his previous books were too complicated for beginning chefs.) And in 2006 he published *Gordon Ramsay's Sunday Lunch*.

A second book produced in October 2006 was an autobiography, which Ramsay entitled *Humble Pie*. In it, he discussed his difficult childhood, his father's alcoholism, and his attempted soccer career. He also told about his experiences in training to try to become the best culinary talent in the world. *Humble Pie* was published at the same time in the United States under the title *Roasting in Hell's Kitchen: Temper Tantrums, F Words, and the Pursuit of Perfection*. The autobiography became a bestseller in the United States and in Great Britain.

Ramsay's culinary tie-ins involved more than cookbooks. In 2006 the temperamental chef announced the release of a new line of merchandise created in partnership with Royal Doulton. Products bearing Gordon Ramsay's name would include dinnerware, glasses, bakeware, and copper-clad and stainless-steel cookware.

During the first season of *The F Word*, Gordon raised turkeys that were named after British television cooks such as Nigella (Lawson), Jamie (Oliver), and Delia (Smith). At the end of the season, the turkeys were butchered and roasted.

AWARDS AND HONORS

Meanwhile, many awards and honors were coming Gordon's way. In 2005 *Ramsay's Kitchen Nightmares* won a British Academy of Film and Television Arts (BAFTA) award for Best Feature. The program also received a 2006 International Emmy for best non-scripted entertainment.

In July 2006 the Queen of England awarded Ramsay an OBE, or Officer of the Order of the British Empire for his services to the hospitality industry. When the office of prime minister Tony Blair had earlier announced the list of people being recognized, it issued a statement explaining the choices: "A key aim was to reward people who really changed things."

Also that July Gordon received the Catey award for Independent Restaurateur of the Year. He had been honored previously with Catey awards, which are the biggest awards of the U.K. hospitality industry. In 1995 he had been recognized as Newcomer of the Year, and in 2000 he received Chef of the Year.

NEW YORK CITY

In 2006, the Blackstone Group wanted a Ramsay restaurant in its London NYC Hotel in New York City, which was being refurbished. It would be Ramsay's 12th restaurant, and his first in the United States. That summer, in between his many commitments, Ramsay was on West 54th Street, Manhattan, helping to start up the restaurant. He selected chef Neil Ferguson to run the $8 million restaurant, and most of its staff came from Ramsay's restaurants in Britain.

In an article in the *New Yorker*, one of the restaurant's staff members commented on how the workers enjoyed Ramsay's presence, despite the chef's reputation for having a fiery temper. An Australian pastry chef named Alistair Wise explained, "We love it when Gordon is here. No politics, no jostling for position—it's his way or the highway, everything decisive."

November 2006 saw the grand opening of Gordon Ramsay at the London NYC. Restaurant critics expected the restaurant would feature dishes that reflected the extreme flair of their creator. Many reviewers expressed disappointment in the mellow feel to both the atmosphere and food. Frank Bruni a food critic for the *New York Times* wrote, "Seldom has a conquistador as bellicose as Mr. Ramsay landed with such a whisper. It's not an unappealing sound, but it's nothing that's going to prick up your ears." The *Times* critic awarded the new restaurant just two out of a possible four stars.

Gordon works in the kitchen of his first restaurant in America, Gordon Ramsay at the London NYC, November 2006.

MORE GROWTH

The relentless expansion of Ramsay's culinary and media empire continued in 2007. That year the third season of *Ramsay's Kitchen Nightmares* and the second season of *The F Word* both aired on Channel 4. In the United States, Ramsay was filming a third season of *Hell's Kitchen* in early 2007, which aired in June.

Gordon also opened several new restaurants. One was in a Blackstone hotel in the exclusive resort town of Boca Raton, Florida. There, Gordon Ramsay at the Cielo opened under the direction of chef Angela Hartnett. Gordon also opened his first pub, The Narrow in Limehouse, and a second pub, The Devonshire in Chiswick, London. And he celebrated a second Michelin star at his restaurant, Petrus.

There was also time that year to publish three new books. Two were cookbooks: *Ramsay's Fast Food: Recipes from the F Word* and *Recipes from a 3 Star Chef*, the latter of which features 50 of his signature dishes from Restaurant Gordon Ramsay. The third book was a followup to his autobiography *Humble Pie. Playing with Fire* details many of Gordon's struggles as he trained to become a chef, launch his first restaurant, and establish himself as the head of a business empire.

A BROTHER'S ADDICTION

A family issue that Gordon first discussed in *Humble Pie* came to an unhappy conclusion in 2007. In the book, Gordon describes his younger brother's problems with drug addiction, which Ronnie blamed on the domestic violence he experienced as a child. "I first saw my father beating my mother when I was only five. It has probably scarred my life," he once told the British newspaper *The Sun*. His sister Diane agreed, noting that Ronnie did not receive the severe beatings that his siblings did. "Instead, Dad would put Ronnie to one side and make him watch a beating. I believe some of that has affected him."

While Gordon used his anger to make something of himself, Ronnie sought to escape from life by using drugs. He was sniffing glue at age 13. In his later teens, he turned to alcohol and drugs. When he was in his twenties, he was hooked on heroin. In the years that followed, Gordon, Tana, and his mother, Helen, tried to help. They gave him money. He and Tana invited Ronnie to live with them. Gordon got him a job in one of his restaurants. And he paid for Ronnie to go through rehabilitation programs several times.

But each time Ronnie quickly relapsed. An exasperated Gordon told an interviewer, "I've been let down so many times. He's stolen from me. . . . I've given him money for haircuts and the next minute he's on his mobile in the middle of King's Cross buying heroin." In *Humble Pie*, Ramsay wrote of his disappointment in finding no solution for Ronnie's addiction, "It's the one thing I feel I've failed at," he admitted. "I find it hard knowing that there's nothing I can do to help."

Then in February 2007 Gordon got word that 39-year-old Ronnie had been arrested in Bali for heroin possession. Ronnie asked Gordon for money to pay a lawyer, but this time Gordon refused. "I had to turn my back on him," he told an interviewer. "[O]therwise I would have been bailing him out knowing that I was part of what got him in there. . . . A distance needs to be created before we can resurrect a relationship. Bt it hurts me and I know deep down inside it must hurt him."

Ronnie could have been imprisoned for 10 years, and he was lucky to be released from prison after only 10 months. He returned to England, but his brother and mother had

Gordon's younger brother, Ronnie Ramsay, is escorted from an Indonesian jail to the courthouse in Denpasar, Bali, where he would stand trial for drug possession. In September 2007, Ronnie was found guilty and sent to prison.

informed him that neither wanted to have anything to do with him. In September 2009 Ronnie was homeless, and photographed living on the streets of London.

U.S. KITCHEN NIGHTMARES

Television commitments in 2007 included the filming of a new program. With the popularity of *Hell's Kitchen*, TV executives for Fox were looking to have Gordon star in another show, this one a U.S. adaptation of the British *Ramsay's Kitchen Nightmares*. In the new show, called *Kitchen Nightmares*, Ramsay has one week to troubleshoot problems and help the managers turn failing restaurants around.

The program first aired in September 2007. In the first episode, Ramsay helped a dysfunctional family-run eatery in

Babylon, New York, Owned by Tina Pelligrino and her brother Peter, who has been mismanaging the Italian restaurant by not putting money into replacing its broken stoves and fixing the walk-in refrigerator. Gordon ultimately introduces a new "family style" menu for the restaurant, renovates the dining area, and provides new stoves and a refrigerator for the kitchen. He also works on changing Peter's attitude so that he is more committed to seeing the restaurant succeed.

Nine more restaurants were visited by Ramsay during Season 1 of *Kitchen Nightmares*. By the time the final episode was aired that December, the new show had a large following. And Fox was ready to sign up Gordon for another season.

CREATING TOP CHEFS

The following statement is posted on the Human Resources webpage of the Gordon Ramsay Holdings site: "At Gordon Ramsay restaurants, we believe in recruiting the best people, equipping them with the skills to shine, the opportunities to develop, and the direction to succeed. It is our employees that make us the best at what we do." The company has provided several ways of developing the talents of its workers. They include:

- Bringing in outside lecturers with specific skills to provide seminars, training, and demonstrations in various areas, such as flower arranging, chocolate making, coffee making, and baking.
- Setting up field trips to various vendors, including wineries, fish markets, and breweries.
- Arranging for employees with specialists experience to share their knowledge, for example, in areas such as wine tasting, butchering, and meat curing.

Among the talented chefs who worked with Ramsay for many years are Angela Hartnett, Marcus Wareing, and Jason Atherton. All reached the top of their career with Ramsay by becoming executive chefs at one or more of his restaurants. Atherton once explained Gordon's philosophy as a boss:

> He's certainly not a nightmare to work for. In fact, he's brilliant because he's straight talking and he helps you move up the ladder. Too many other chefs are threatened by talented, younger staff, but if Gordon sees a talented chef he takes them under his wing and then, when they are ready to fly, gives them their own restaurant.

NAME THE INGREDIENTS

Gordon Ramsay requires all his chefs to pass a certain test before they can be promoted. After being blindfolded, they are given various foods, which they must be able to identify by taste alone. If they know what it is they are eating, they're eligible for promotion.

Gordon learned from Guy Savoy in Paris years ago that a master chef must have an appreciation of taste and flavor. So Ramsay expects his employees to have the ability to know how foods taste in order to know how to blend the best flavors together. "The easiest way for a new chef to impress me is with their seasoning," he explains. "It sounds obvious doesn't it? A bit of pepper and salt. But that gives me a real indication of what a cook's palate is like. You could be the most able cook when it comes to roasting a scallop or braising a turbot, but if you can't season what you're doing, you're lost."

EIGHT RESTAURANTS IN 2008

In 2008 Gordon Ramsay Holdings acquired Tante Marie's Cooking School. Graduating chefs would have no shortage of Gordon's restaurants to apply to, as he opened eight more restaurants worldwide that year.

Two were in Versailles, France—Gordon Ramsay au Trianon and La Veranda. One was a bistro in the Chelsea section of London called Foxtrot Oscar. Another new restaurant in London was Maze Grill at the Marriott. Still another was Gordon Ramsay at the London West Hollywood, in California. One was even at an airport—with Stuart Gillies, Ramsay launched Gordon Ramsay Plane Food, a restaurant located in Terminal 5 of London's Heathrow Airport. Yet another was the fine-dining restaurant, Murano, opened in London's Mayfair. It was headed by Angela Hartnett.

MORE BOOKS AND TV

Ramsay also published two more cookbooks. *Cooking for Friends: Food from My Table* and *Healthy Appetite* were both released on 2008. The latter book features more than 100 recipes for healthy breakfasts, lunches, dinners, and desserts,

Although Gordon Ramsay decided not to participate in the ITV version of *Hell's Kitchen* after the first season in 2004, the program was not canceled. Instead, later seasons of *Hell's Kitchen* in the U.K. featured several different top chefs. One of them was Gordon's former mentor, Marco Pierre White. He appeared on Season 3 (2007) and Season 4 (2009).

and it gives information on how to cook for both health and flavor.

Life remained hectic as television commitments found Gordon filming fourth seasons of *The F Word* and the U.S. version of *Hell's Kitchen*. He also appeared in 2008 in a special called *Gordon Ramsay's Cookalong Live*, which aired on Channel 4. In the program, he shows viewers and a live studio audience how to prepare some of his dishes.

Gordon was extremely wealthy in 2008. His television work was bringing in millions of dollars. And he owned more than 20 restaurants around the world, which were worth more than $80 million.

Gordon's success in America led the Fox network to develop new shows for the chef/entrepreneur.

Gordon serves a vegetable curry to the Malaysian prime minister, Najib Tun Razak, during filming for the ITV program Gordon's Great Escape in Kuala Lumpur, June 2011. The show saw Ramsey explore the culinary traditions of southeast Asia through visits to Thailand, Cambodia, Malaysia, and Vietnam.

CHAPTER EIGHT

A CHALLENGING FUTURE

Although his busy television schedule often kept Ramsay on the road seven months out of the year, he tried hard to maintain ties with his children. In a June 2008 interview in *People* magazine, he talked about how he enjoys his son and three daughters, particularly when it comes to introducing them to new foods. "They've eaten lamb's brains," he boasted. "Yeah! They loved them."

FAMILY MAN

Because he grew up with a father who was harsh and unstable, Gordon has sought balance in parenting, he told the magazine reporter. He tries to be both a friend to his children as well as a firm disciplinarian. As they have grown up, they have had to follow certain rules such as television only on weekends, no candy or desserts after school, and no swearing (despite their father's own frequent use of curse words on television).

But Gordon's efforts to provide a happy environment for the Ramsay family were shaken in November 2008 when author Sarah Symonds claimed that she had been having a seven-year affair with the chef. He denied the allegation. Some of Tana's friends advised her to leave Gordon, but she chose to believe her husband and stayed with him.

Later, Tana explained that she never doubted her husband, but that the couple were "battered and bruised" by the accusation. She assured an interviewer, "We have an amazingly close relationship, amazing trust and loyalty, and that hasn't changed in any way, shape or form."

FINANCIAL FAILINGS

As 2008 came to a close, the profits from Gordon's restaurant empire suddenly fell drastically, and Gordon Ramsay Holdings failed to meet its obligations on a loan from the Royal Bank of Scotland. The troubles were blamed on the weakening world economy. But the business model was also part of the problem: the company owned most of its restaurants, which meant it was responsible for everything from rent to salaries. It soon became clear that all of Gordon's overseas restaurants were losing money. The New York restaurant alone had losses of $4 million a year.

An auditing firm warned that Ramsay Gordon Holdings had grown too quickly, increasing from 45 employees in 1998 to 1,250 in 2009. The firm called on Ramsay to declare bankruptcy. But he refused, and spent the next few months trying to come up with a better solution. "Everything was on the line," he later told Bloomberg. "December, January, February and March were the most highly pressurized . . . most awful four months I've ever had in business."

Ultimately, Ramsay chose to close a few restaurants, and he and his CEO, Chris Hutcheson, transferred millions of dollars from their personal funds into the company. (Ramsay

A 2008 photo of the Ramsay family at a movie premiere. That year the family was rocked by allegations that Gordon had an affair, which he denied.

Tana Ramsay has published several cookbooks. The first, *Tana Ramsay's Family Kitchen*, came out in 2006. She has also published *Tana Ramsay's Real Family Food* (2007) and *Tana Ramsay's Kitchen Secrets* (2010).

held a 69 percent share and Hutcheson a 31 percent share.) Gordon also restructured the business, renegotiating contracts with Blackstone so the firm assumed ownership of its hotel restaurants and paid Ramsay a consulting fee to run them. Through these efforts, he hoped to help the company rebound.

ECONOMIC DOWNTURN

Ramsay in 2009 was one of the highest earning chefs in the world, with an estimated fortune of around $95 million. But most of that came from his television deals, cookbooks, and licensing agreements. His restaurants continued to drain the company.

Ramsay has admitted that expanding his restaurant empire in 2008 and 2009 was not good for his business. "I opened 12 restaurants in 15 months heading into the recession, when in hindsight I should have been tightening my belt," he said later. "When the recession hit . . . I'd just hired 350 staff in Paris, plus 500 staff in New York and LA." Although business was good in the U.K., he had large losses overseas.

As a result, Ramsay had to restructure his debts. This involved giving up ownership of his hotel restaurants to the hotels, and he now receives a consulting fee. "All businesses have taken a huge hit in the last 18 months," he explained in early 2011. "Business-wise I didn't panic—I've been in more high-pressure situations in my life. But on a personal level, I did become more thick-skinned. Every . . . columnist came out of the woodwork with an opinion. I've stopped reading that stuff. You have to, because it drives you mad. It's made me more determined to be successful."

Despite its financial problems, Gordon Ramsay Holdings continued to open a few restaurants. It launched three international restaurants—in Cape Town, South Africa, in 2009; and in Melbourne, Australia, and Doha, Qatar, in 2010. And in November 2010, the company relaunched The Savoy Grill in London. In the summer of 2011, Ramsay opened his first restaurant in Canada, Laurier Gordon Ramsay, located in Montreal. Gordon Ramsay Holdings has been recovering, Ramsay tells interviewers.

During the economic downturn, Gordon continued to command top salaries with his increasing load of television work. He was busy in the U.K. that year filming episodes of *The F Word* and in 2009 a new program called *Gordon's Great Escape*. As of 2011 nine seasons of *Hell's Kitchen* had been filmed in the United States.

Another dependable source of income for Ramsay's company are merchandising deals. In 2009, he launched a line of

In March 2009 Ramsay was awarded two Michelin stars for his Gordon Ramsay au Trianon, in Versailles. This made him the first British chef to have a two-star restaurant in France. It also brought his total of Michelin stars to 12.

Despite the economic hard times, Gordon continued opening new restaurants. Here, he prepares food at his Maze restaurant in Cape Town, South Africa, which opened in April 2009.

Gordon Ramsay Professional kitchenware. The line included electrical appliances such as toasters, blenders, toaster ovens, and coffee makers—all bearing the Ramsay name. September 2011 saw the launch of a new line of Ramsay kitchenware, which includes cookware, knives, blenders, coffee makers, and utensils. The merchandise is sold through the retail store Kmart and online.

CHEF TURNOVER

As the restaurant side of Gordon Ramsay Holdings faltered, some of Ramsay's top chefs left the company to strike out on their own. One was Marcus Wareing, who had a public split with Ramsay in the spring of 2009. Wareing and Ramsay had worked together for 19 years as business partners and friends. When Marcus, who was operating Petrus at the Berkeley Hotel, announced he planned to branch out on his own, a bitter legal dispute over the ownership of Petrus followed. Ultimately, Ramsay kept the restaurant name, while Wareing remained in the same building. He renamed the new restaurant Marcus Wareing at the Berkeley, and in March 2010 Gordon reopened Petrus at a nearby location.

Another Ramsay protégé to move on was Jason Atherton. He had served as executive chef of the Maze restaurants until April 2010. A month later he opened his own restaurant in Shanghai, China.

Angela Hartnett left in October 2010 by buying out Murano from Gordon Ramsay Holdings. She had headed this restaurant since it opened in 2008 and left on good terms with Gordon. Ramsay would later blame the loss of so many of the company's top chefs on Chris Hutcheson's failure to reward them financially.

FAMILY FEUD

Ramsay had far greater complaints to make about his father-in-law and company CEO. Gordon Ramsay Holdings was continuing to have serious financial problems, with reports of debts as high as 17 million pounds, or $27 million. And the company was being hit with lawsuits from multiple creditors.

In October 2010, Gordon, who has a majority share in Gordon Ramsay Holdings, fired Hutcheson from the company. At the time he accused Hutcheson of misusing company funds. Ramsay also made the shocking revelation that Hutcheson had used the money he took to support a second family, complete with two grown children, that he had with a mistress.

The accusations led Chris and Greta Hutcheson to cut off all ties with Gordon and their daughter Tana. The following month, Greta, wrote a letter to Tana telling her to leave Ramsay. In response, Gordon published an open letter to his mother-in-law in the *London Evening Standard*, in which he asked her not to sever links with the Ramsay family. Meanwhile, Chris Hutcheson filed a lawsuit against his son-in-law for unfair dismissal. Greta, her son Adam, and grand-son—all of whom had worked for the company—also filed lawsuits against Ramsay.

In August 2011, Gordon filed his own lawsuit, in which he alleged that Chris Hutcheson had hacked into Gordon's per-

In January 2011 Gordon celebrated ten years of Restaurant Gordon Ramsay in Chelsea holding three Michelin stars.

sonal and business e-mails and files, as well as taken large sums of money that did not belong to him. The family rift has been difficult for Gordon and Tana, who subsequently released a statement saying they would let the legal process take its course.

Ramsay continued to make a great deal of money from lucrative licensing deals and his ever-expanding television career. But increasing commitments to U.S. television shows meant that he had to spend more time in the United States. He rented a mansion in Hollywood Hills, California, for the family, although Tana and the children continued to live most of the time at their home in London.

One of Gordon's closest friends is British soccer star David Beckham. The Ramsay and Beckham children are about the same age and often play together when the families are on vacation.

MASTERCHEF

The popularity of his two Fox hits led to an offer for Gordon to host a third program. Production of the new reality show, which is an amateur cooking competition called *MasterChef*, began airing in July 2010.

Thousands of amateur cooks auditioned for the show, and 100 of them were invited to prepare a signature dish for three judges—Gordon Ramsay, Joe Bastianich, and Graham

Gordon poses with fellow MasterChef judges Joe Bastianich (left) and Graham Elliot. Bastianich owns several restaurants, as well as wineries in Italy and Argentina. Elliot is a Michelin star-winning chef from Chicago. A third season of MasterChef will air in 2012.

Elliott. In this show, Ramsay serves more as a mentor, and not so much a bully, to the aspiring chefs. His experience in teaching his own children how to cook, he says, has made it easier for him to be more nurturing to the group. Over the course of the *MasterChef* season, the judges eliminated contestants, with the winner of the competition receiving $250,000 as well as a cookbook contract.

MasterChef was another hit for Ramsay, who was signed on for a second season. In 2010 Fox network also broadcast seasons seven and eight of *Hell's Kitchen*, and the third season of *Kitchen Nightmares*. The three U.S. shows paid Gordon an estimated $15 million a year.

Ramsay also created his own production company called One Potato Two Potato, in which he partnered with Optomen Television. It is based in London, but in the summer of 2010 the company opened an office in Los Angeles. One Potato Two Potato produced the holiday special *Christmas with Gordon*, which aired on Channel 4 in December. And it was responsible for the production of *MasterChef*, which was its first U.S. series.

BIG FISH FIGHT

In January 2011, Ramsay teamed up with British chefs Heston Blumenthal and Jamie Oliver on a Channel 4 series called *Big Fish Fight*. In it, the three chefs presented programs dealing with the worldwide problem of overfishing and the threatened extinction of certain species of fish. Ramsay told a reporter with the *Daily Mail*, "We're fighting against greed and overindulgence," he said. "Chefs are part of the problem. We're responsible for making people want certain fish."

Gordon's part of the program investigated the illegal trade in shark fins, which are used to make shark fin soup, a delicacy in China, or are dried and sold for as much as $300 per pound. It is an unregulated, multibillion-dollar industry. But the method of harvesting the shark fins is controversial. "How they do it is quite upsetting," Gordon explained. "They shock [the shark] with an electric prod, but the shark's still moving while they cut it up and throw it back dying into the water." Many nations are considering banning the practice.

Ramsay's investigation took him to Costa Rica, where he was involved in dangerous confrontations with men working in the shark fin trade. He explained,

> [G]angs operate from places that are like forts, with barbed-wire perimeters and gun towers. At one, I managed to shake off the people who were keeping us away, ran up some stairs to a rooftop and looked down to see thousands and thousands of fins, drying on rooftops for as far as the eye could see. When I got back downstairs, they tipped a barrel of petrol over me.

Ramsay escaped from being set on fire, but another investigation aboard a fishing boat led to a potentially deadly situation. Gordon's crew was filming when he found a hidden bag of freshly cut fins. That discovery resulted in threats to their lives. "Back at the wharf, there were people pointing rifles at us to stop us filming," he said. "A van pulled up and these seedy characters made us stand against a wall." The timely arrival of Costa Rican police prevented any violence, but Ramsay and his investigative team were advised to leave the country, he told reporters.

OUT OF THE KITCHEN

Gordon's television success in the United States brought him yet another franchise. In September 2011 Fox announced it

At the 2011 People's Choice Awards, Hell's Kitchen was nominated for Favorite Competition Show, and Gordon Ramsay was nominated for Favorite TV Chef.

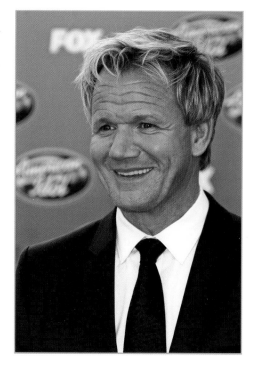

would be airing Ramsay's fourth reality TV show with the network. The new program was modeled on *Kitchen Nightmares*, and given the working title of *Hotel Hell*. It was reported that the chef would be leaving the kitchen to do some troubleshooting for struggling hotels, motels, and bed and breakfasts across the United States. Ramsay would also serve as executive producer of the show, and his company One Potato Two Potato would produce it.

Whatever Ramsay does, he brings his best efforts to the table. The words he wrote about himself years ago in his autobiography continue to hold true:

> I'm as driven as any man you'll ever meet. I can't ever sit still. . . . I just keep going, moving as far away as possible from where I began. Where am I trying to get to: I wonder. . . .Work is who I am, who I want to be. I sometimes think that if I were to stop, I'd cease to exist.

CHAPTER NOTES

p. 7: "Chef Ramsay is going . . ." *Hell's Kitchen: Season 4 Raw & Uncensored*, DVD, Episode 401. Millennium Media Solutions, 2010.

p. 9: "How do you react . . ." Erin Gaughan, "HK9CastingApplicationFinal," The Conlin Company (October 25, 2010).

p. 9: "They locked me . . ." Edward Wyatt, "TV Contestants: Tired, Tipsy and Pushed to Brink," *New York Times* (August 2, 2009), p. A1.

p. 11: "Who cooked the chicken? . . ." *Hell's Kitchen: Season 4*, Episode 401.

p. 11: "Get dressed. Go . . ." *Hell's Kitchen: Season 4*. Episode 402.

p. 12: "Now every rubber chicken . . ." *Hell's Kitchen: Season 4*, Episode 402.

p. 16: "I watched how he . . ." Gordon Ramsay, "Ramsay: No One Should Suffer Abuse Like My Mum," CNN Living (September 25, 2007). http://articles.cnn.com/2007-09-25/living/ramsay.commentary_1_domestic-violence-role-model-charity?_s=PM:LIVING

p. 16: "As a boy, I was . . ." Gordon Ramsay, *Humble Pie* (London: Harper Collins Entertainment, 2006), p. 10.

p.16: "Ronnie was always . . ." Neil Simpson, *Gordon Ramsay: The Biography* (London: John Blake Publishing, 2006), p. 17.

p.19: "I said no, straight away . . ." Ibid., p. 25.

p.19: "I went home, sat down . . ." Ibid., pp. 25–26.

p. 19: "I loved it instantly . . ." Ibid., p. 29.

p. 21: "There was nothing like it . . ." Sarah Lyall, "The Terrible-Tempered Star Chef of London," *The New York Times* (February 23, 2005). http://www.nytimes.com/2005/02/23/dining/23gord.html

p.21: "I was obsessed with . . ." Simpson, *Gordon Ramsay: The Biography*, p. 29.

p. 22: "I want to go . . ." Sandra Laville, "The Guardian Profile: Gordon Ramsay," *The Guardian* (May 28, 2004). http://www.guardian.co.uk/media/2004/may/28/realitytv.broadcasting

p. 23: "In the beginning, I . . ." Ramsay, *Humble Pie*, p. 78.

p. 24: "The trick is . . ." Simpson, *Gordon Ramsay: The Biography*, p. 38.

p. 25: "a nation of culinary barbarians . . ." Ibid., p. 39.

p. 26: "You're in a house . . ." Ramsay, quoted in Lyall, "The Terrible-Tempered Star Chef of London."

p. 26: "In Paris, I learned . . ." Ramsay, *Humble Pie*, p. 100.

p. 26: "One of the many things . . ." Simpson, *Gordon Ramsay: The Biography*, pp. 40–41.

p. 27: "Robuchon was such an unpleasant . . ." Ramsay, *Humble Pie*, p. 112.

p. 28: "one star: a very good . . ." "The Michelin Guide: 100 Editions and Over a Century of History," ViaMichelin (March 2, 2009). http://www.viamichelin.co.uk/tpl/mag6/art200903/htm/tour-saga-michelin.htm

p. 29: "I wanted to learn . . ." Simpson, *Gordon Ramsay: The Biography*, p. 42.

p. 29: "The two and half years . . ." Ibid., p. 43.

p. 30: "I kept my imaginary restaurant . . ." Ramsay, *Humble Pie*, p. 128.

p. 31: "He was an animal . . ." William Green, "Gordon Ramsay Flees Kitchen as TV Fame Saves Restaurant Empire," Bloomberg (December 10, 2009). http://www.bloomberg.com/apps/news?pid=newsarchive&sid=aRE.WJ51Hq2s

p. 31: "[Ramsay] was there at seven . . ." Carole Cadwalladr, "Ramsay's Kitchen Queen," *The Guardian* (April 28, 2007). http://www.guardian.co.uk/lifeandstyle/2007/apr/29/foodanddrink.features9

p. 32: "Minutes later, I found out . . ." Bill Buford, "The Taming of the Chef," *New Yorker* (April 4, 2007). http://www.newyorker.com/reporting/2007/04/02/070402fa_fact_buford#

p. 34: "He just said, 'It's such . . ." Simpson, *Gordon Ramsay: The Biography*, p. 62.

p. 34: "[S]he knew what it . . ." Ramsay, *Humble Pie*, p.143.

p. 36: "I would have had to . . ." Simpson, *Gordon Ramsay: The Biography*, p. 66.

p. 39: "You're more than welcome to . . ." Ramsay, *Humble Pie*, p. 164.

p. 40: "We had 52 people in . . ." Simpson, *Gordon Ramsay: The Biography*, p. 70.

p. 42:   "People said I threw him . . ." Ibid., p. 87.

p. 42:   "It was as if we . . ." Ibid., p.73.

p. 43:   "No one should die . . ." Ibid., p.74.

p. 43:   "My father taught me . . ." Celia Dodd, "Gordon Ramsay Loves the Simple Life," *The Times* (April 18, 2008). http://women.timesonline.co.uk/tol/life_and_style/women/celebrity/article3771418.ece

p. 45:   "All I am using is . . ." Simpson, *Gordon Ramsay: The Biography*, pp.79–80.

p. 45:   "I'm doing it for . . ." Ibid., p. 89.

p. 48:   "Ramsay's food is vibrant . . ." Ibid., p. 96.

p. 52:   "A monster has arrived in . . ." Ibid., pp.118–119.

p. 55:   "He was not . . ." "Ramsay Speaks at Chef's Inquest," BBC News (July 9, 2003). http://news.bbc.co.uk/2/hi/uk_news/england/london/3052399.stm

p. 56:   "People say you need drugs . . ." Simpson, *Gordon Ramsay: The Biography*, p.157.

p. 57:   "I am completely shocked . . ." Lorraine Fisher, "Gordon Ramsay's No1 Chef Dies Burgling Flat," *The Mirror* (May 9, 2003).

p. 57:   We have zero tolerance . . ." Simpson, *Gordon Ramsay: The Biography*, p. 155.

p. 60:   "I thought it would be . . ." Simpson, Ibid., p.111.

p. 60:   "[H]e may be a . . ." "Gordon Ramsay: Chef Terrible," BBC News (July 20, 2001). http://news.bbc.co.uk/2/hi/uk_news/1448742.stm

p. 61:   "Gordon is actually . . ." Simpson, *Gordon Ramsay: The Biography*, p.114.

p. 62:   "The places we visit . . ." Ramsay, *Humble Pie*, p. 259.

p. 64:   " You will have to sweep . . ." Simpson, *Gordon Ramsay: The Biography*, pp. 175–176.

p. 64:   "The real problem with the show . . ." Ramsay, *Humble Pie*, pp. 265–266.

p. 66:   "He's world-renowned . . ." Simpson, *Gordon Ramsay: The Biography*, p. 249.

p. 68:   "I've been cooking . . ." Lyall, "The Terrible-Tempered Star Chef of London."

p. 68:   "He's a perfectionist . . ." Lyall, "The Terrible-Tempered Star Chef of London."

p. 68:   "I have a normal . . ." Lyall, "The Terrible-Tempered Star Chef of London."

p. 69:   "The problem with Yanks is . . ." Simpson, *Gordon Ramsay: The Biography*, p. 254.

p. 69:   "I'd just like to say . . ." Nicola Methven, "Ramsay
         Apology to Collins," *The Mirror* (November 2, 2005).
         http://www.mirror.co.uk/news/tm_objectid=16320605&me
         thod=full&siteid=115875&headline=ramsay-apology-to-
         collins-name_page.html
p. 71:   "I have always hated . . ." Simpson, *Gordon Ramsay: The
         Biography*, p. 266.
p. 72:   "The same person who is . . ." Ibid., p. 271.
p. 74:   "A key aim was . . ." Reed V. Landberg, "U.K. Honors
         London Terror Attack Heroes, Executives, Athletes,"
         Bloomberg (December 30, 2005).
         http://www.bloomberg.com/apps/news?pid=newsarchive&s
         id=aqtQSnesXm5A&refer=uk
p. 75:   "We love it when Gordon . . ." Bill Buford,"The Taming of
         the Chef," *New Yorker* (April 4, 2007).
         http://www.newyorker.com/reporting/2007/04/02/070402f
         a_fact_buford#
p. 75:   "seldom has a conquistador . . ." Frank Bruni, "For a Bad
         Boy Chef, He's Certainly Polite," *The New York Times*
         (January 31, 2007).
         http://www.nytimes.com/2007/01/31/dining/reviews/31rest
         .html?pagewanted=all
p. 76:   "I first saw my father . . ." S. Hendry, "Ramsay Mum on
         Son's Drug Hell," *The Sun*.
         http://www.thesun.co.uk/sol/homepage/news/25396/Rams
         ay-mum-on-sons-drug-hell.html?print=yes
p. 77:   "Instead, Dad would put Ronnie . . ." Ibid.
p. 77:   "I've been let down . . ." Simpson, *Gordon Ramsay: The
         Biography*, p.105–106.
p. 77:   "It's the one thing . . ." Ramsay, *Humble Pie*.
p. 77:   "I had to turn my . . ." Dodd, "Gordon Ramsay Loves the
         Simple Life."
p. 79:   "At Gordon Ramsay restaurants . . ." "Gordon Ramsay—
         Learning & Development," Gordon Ramsay (May 2,
         2006). http://www.gordonramsay.com/corporate/humanre-
         sources/learninganddevelopment/
p. 80:   "He's certainly not a nightmare . . ." Simpson, *Gordon
         Ramsay: The Biography*, p. 130.
p. 80:   "The easiest way . . ." Ramsay, *Humble Pie*, p. 192.
p. 85:   "They've eaten lamb's brains. . . ." Kate Stroup,"At Home
         with Gordon Ramsay," *People* (June 23, 2008).
         http://www.people.com/people/archive/arti-
         cle/0,,20207200.html
p. 86:   "battered and bruised" Louette Harding, "Why I Didn't

Doubt Gordon Ramsay," *Daily Mail Online* (April 19, 2010). http://www.dailymail.co.uk/home/you/article-1265706/Why-I-didnt-doubt-Gordon-Tana-Ramsay.html

p. 86: "We have an amazingly . . ." Ibid.

p. 86: "Everything was on the . . ." Green, "Gordon Ramsay Flees Kitchen as TV Fame Saves Restaurant Empire."

p. 88: "I opened 12 restaurants . . ." Simon Lewis, "Who's the Reel Deal? Heston Blumenthal, Gordon Ramsay and Jamie Oliver take on the Villains of the Fishing World," *Daily Mail Online* (January 5, 2011). http://www.daily-mail.co.uk/home/moslive/article-1343055/Jamie-Oliver-Gordon-Ramsay-Heston-Blumenthal-villains-fishing-world.html

p. 88: "All businesses have taken . . ." Ibid.

p. 95: "We're fighting against . . ." Ibid.

p. 96: "How they do it . . ." Ibid.

p. 96: "[G]angs operate from places . . ." Ibid.

p. 96: "Back at the wharf, there . . ." Ibid.

p. 97: "I'm as driven as . . ." Ramsay, *Humble Pie*, p. 10.

CHRONOLOGY

1966: On November 8 Gordon Ramsay is born in Johnstone, Renfrewshire, Scotland.

1984: While training to become a professional soccer player with the Glasgow Rangers, Gordon injures his knee; the following year he is cut from the team and pursues a cooking career.

1986: Ramsay begins working for chef Marco Pierre White.

1987: Ramsay receives an HND in hotel management at North Oxon Technical Catering College; trains with world-renowned French chef Guy Savoy in Paris.

1993: Ramsay returns to London, where on October 10 he opens Aubergine as head chef and part-owner.

1995: Gordon receives his first Michelin star as head chef at Aubergine.

1996: Ramsay publishes his first cookbook, *Passion for Flavour*. In December, he marries Cayetana "Tana" Hutchinson.

1998: In September Gordon opens his own place, Restaurant Gordon Ramsay, in Chelsea.

1999: Ramsay gains fame with the Channel 4 broadcast of the documentary *Boiling Point*; opens Petrus with Marcus Wareing in Mayfair.

2001: Restaurant Gordon Ramsay is awarded its third Michelin star.

CHRONOLOGY

2004: Two television programs, *Ramsay's Kitchen Nightmares* and *Hell's Kitchen*, premiere in the United Kingdom.

2005: In May, the first episode of the U.S. version of *Hell's Kitchen* is broadcast on Fox; *The F Word* debuts on Channel 4 in the U.K.

2006: In July, Ramsay is appointed OBE; in October, his autobiography, *Humble Pie*, is published in the U.K. In November, his first U.S. restaurant, Gordon Ramsay at the London NYC opens.

2007: In September, *Kitchen Nightmares* premieres in the United States.

2009: Profits at Gordon Ramsay Holdings fall.

2010: Fox begins broadcasting the reality cooking show *MasterChef*.

2011: Restaurant Gordon Ramsay celebrates 10 years of holding 3 Michelin stars; Fox announces Ramsay's involvement in a fourth reality TV program with the working title *Hotel Hell*.

GLOSSARY

AUBERGINE—the British term for eggplant; also used to describe the dark purple color of an eggplant.

BISTRO—a small, unpretentious restaurant.

CUISINE—a style or method of cooking.

CULINARY—having to do with cooking and the kitchen.

ENTRÉE—the main dish or course.

GOURMET—related to the preparation of high-quality food that is sophisticated, expensive, rare, or carefully prepared; or, a person devoted to the consumption of fine food and drink.

HAUTE CUISINE—the preparation and cooking of high quality food, typically in the style of traditional French cuisine.

HORS D'OEUVRE—a small savory dish, usually served as an appetizer before a meal.

MAÎTRE D'—a person in a restaurant who oversees the wait staff and handles reservations.

MENTOR—a person who guides and directs another person along a career path.

PALATE—a person's appreciation of taste and flavor.

PROTÉGÉ—a person who is guided and supported by a more experienced person, or mentor.

REALITY TV—an unscripted television program.

SHAREHOLDER—a person who owns a share, or part, of a property or fund.

SOUS CHEF—a chef in a restaurant who is second in authority below the head chef.

Ramsay, Gordon. *A Chef for All Seasons*. London: Quadrille, 2010.

———. *Cooking for Friends*. New York: William Morrow, 2008.

———. *Healthy Appetite*. Toronto: Key Porter Books, 2008.

———. *Playing with Fire*. London: John Blake Publishing, 2007.

———. *Roasting in Hell's Kitchen: Temper Tantrums, F Words, and the Pursuit of Perfection*. New York: Harper Collins Entertainment, 2006.

———. *Three-Star Chef*. Toronto: Key Porter Books, 2008.

———. *World Kitchen*. Toronto: Key Porter Books, 2010.

Simpson, Neil. *Gordon Ramsay: The Biography*. London: John Blake Publishing, 2006.

INTERNET RESOURCES

HTTP://WWW.GORDONRAMSAY.COM

Gordon's exclusive homepage serves up the latest news and information on Ramsay, his restaurants, merchandise, books, and career opportunities with his company.

HTTP://WWW.FOX.COM/HELLSKITCHEN/BIOS/JUDGE/ GORDON-RAMSAY

The Fox Broadcasting Company's website for *Hell's Kitchen* includes information about Gordon Ramsay's popular show, and offers numerous video clips, cooking tips, and photos.

HTTP://WWW.FOX.COM/MASTERCHEF

On this website devoted to the TV show *MasterChef* are links to full episodes of the program, as well as information on contestants, and a forum for discussing the show.

HTTP://WWW.CHANNEL4.COM/4FOOD

The website for the British network Channel 4 includes news, information, and recipes by Ramsay and other British chefs.

HTTP://WWW.BBCGOODFOOD.COM/CONTENT/RECIPES/ FAVOURITES/GORDON-RAMSAY

This BBC website offers a variety of Ramsay's recipes rated by ease of preparation.

Publisher's Note: The websites listed on these pages were active at the time of publication. The publisher is not responsible for websites that have changed their address or discontinued operation since the date of publication.

Numbers in **bold italics** refer to captions.

CONTRIBUTORS

Have you ever been around someone who loves to take notes? Ask her to write a short paragraph and she's filled up a page? Well, that's ANNETTE GALIOTO. One of those crazy people who would rather play scrabble than watch TV. From her home at the base of a mountain, Galioto shares her life with two horses, three cats, a dog, and a lizard. In between feeding, brushing, walking, bathing, training, and being a slave to them, she happily shuffles words around.

Photo credits: Associated Press: 78; FilmMagic: 70; Getty Images: 23, 33, 51, 63, 75, 84, 87, 90; Gerry Penny/AFP/Getty Images: 40, 44; Gamma-Rapho via Getty Images: 53; courtesy Monte Carlo Tourist Bureau: 27; Fox/Photofest: 7, 10, 66, 68, 94; used under license from Shutterstock.com: 9, 15, 80; DSPA / Shutterstock.com: 18; Helga Esteb / Shutterstock.com: 12; Featureflash / Shutterstock.com: 58, 83; Joe Seer / Shutterstock.com: 93, 97; posztos (color-lab.hu) / Shutterstock.com: 28; Rachael Russell / Shutterstock.com: 56; worldswildlifewonders / Shutterstock.com: 54; WireImage: 46.

Cover images: photo by Chris Jackson/Getty Images (portrait); used under license from Shutterstock.com (collage).